Christ in Practice

Also by Clive Marsh
CHRIST IN FOCUS

Christ in Practice

A Christology of Everyday Life

CLIVE MARSH

DARTON·LONGMAN +TODD

First published in 2006 by
Darton, Longman and Todd Ltd
1 Spencer Court
140-142 Wandsworth High Street
London SW18 4JJ

ISBN 0 232 52541 2

A catalogue record for this book is available from the British Library.

Printed and bound in Great Britain by
CPI Bath

To

Alice
Andrew
Becky
Chris
Jonathan
Mandy
Miranda
Oliver
Penny
Rachel
Ruth
Samuel
Sarah
Vaughan

a dispersed community of practice

Contents

Preface

This book has taken over ten years to complete, even though the basic questions it is addressing, and its conclusions, are really quite simple. The questions I have been asking during this time are set out at the start of my related book *Christ in Focus: Radical Christocentrism in Christian Theology* (SCM Press):

> What do Christians mean when they say 'Jesus is here'? What does the attempt to be 'Christ-like' actually amount to? What does it mean to claim to be 'in Christ', or to say that 'Jesus Christ is with us'? What sense can be attached to the Church's identification of itself as the 'body of Christ'? And is the Church the only 'body of Christ' in the world today?

Of course, one reason why the two-volume project has taken so long to complete is that these questions are not easy to answer. More importantly, real life (helpfully) got in the way. I never thought, in any case, that it would be possible to answer the questions in the form of an academic project or as a result of 'church-based' reflection. Yet I did not foresee quite how much 'real life' would become interwoven with the conclusions I have reached.

What follows is not a dispassionate academic account of Christology. Nor is it a straightforward statement of Christian orthodoxy. I have not set out to be unorthodox. I have simply tried not to expound merely what 'must' be said 'according to the tradition'. The book is thus more experimental and exploratory than a doctrine text might be. I am not writing mere autobiography, even if life-experience is woven into the account. Nor am I offering a statement of what I would like Christ to be like. I have engaged with Christian tradition throughout.

So what *is* this book, then? It is a practical Christology. It is an exposition of the meaning of Christ as discovered through, and related to, the practice of human living. In it I attempt to clarify how what Christians make of Jesus Christ helps us understand what it means to be a human being. It is therefore a handbook for

Christians in the present. It also constitutes a challenge to anyone of a different religious tradition or of none to think about how *their* understanding of what it means to be human is gained and 'worked with' – what stories they live by. The context and focus of the work are Western, because of who I am and where I live, though I trust that my findings and insights might be useful in many other places.

Why have I written the book? Why did I start with all those questions in the first place? Simply because I became dissatisfied with the sloppy, lazy way in which Christians often use their language. It is much too easy, 'inside' a religious tradition, to assume that 'we all know what we mean' by phrases we use. *Of course* there are 'insider' and 'outsider' perspectives in religion. And 'insider language' – be it the poetry of prayer or liturgy, or technicalities of theology – may not immediately communicate its meaning to those outside a particular religious discourse. But something is wrong when believers baffle *each other* with terms they use. I kept hearing Christians referring to 'Jesus' and 'Christ' in many diverse and perplexing ways, conveying all sorts of different ideas, and I thought it was time to take a closer look. I have tried to tease out what Christians are trying to say and do with their statements about Jesus/the Christ.

I have both scrutinized the way that human life is lived and conducted conversations with the Bible and theological tradition. The two interlinked strands of enquiry have proved equally important. The first book of the two, *Christ in Focus*, could be regarded as the more 'systematic', and this present volume as the more 'practical', but describing the two books as such neat packages would be slightly misleading. *Christ in Focus* admittedly contains three extended discussions with theologians (Schleiermacher, Rauschenbusch and Brock) and this volume only one (Bonhoeffer). Yet all four conversations have influenced the whole project, and biblical material has been wrestled with throughout. So I resist the notions that thinking and living can remain separate, and that systematic theology is about thinking while practical theology is about living.

That said, you are starting to read a book about Christian practice. Indeed, you might want to move straight into the heart of what makes this book different from many books about

Christology – its exploration of Christ as 'community of practice' – and in that case you could begin at Chapter 2. I do hope, though, that once you have read the rest of the book you will return both to the more theoretical Chapter 1 and to *Christ in Focus*, so that you appreciate the project as a whole. In that way you will gain a fuller grasp of what I believe to be the importance of Christology, not just for Christianity, but for human living.

Acknowledgements

The many people thanked in my earlier book, *Christ in Focus*, deserve to be thanked again. Even though most have not read a word of this present text, conversations with them, or their comments on drafts of that companion volume, have fed into this one. So, thank you once more. Among those with whom I have especially valued contact and conversation in recent years, in addition to the fourteen to whom the book is dedicated, I must mention Richard Clutterbuck, Jane Craske, Neil Stubbens and Martin Wellings. They, along with other members past and present of the Faith and Order Committee of the Methodist Church in Great Britain, remind me from a variety of theological perspectives how and why theological enquiry is crucial for a lively faith and church. I would also like to thank Virginia Hearn and the staff at DLT for taking the book on and seeing it through the necessary stages of production.

My main expression of gratitude, though, is to Ruth Nason. One of the happiest occurrences in my professional life in the past five years has been to team up with Ruth. For years, editors had tipped me off that I needed to find someone who could help me with my writing, so that ideas could be polished more before they reached publishers, and my over-elaborate academic style could be toned down. Ruth has now helped me in this way on three books. She says all the things that need to be said in a forthright but supportive and constructive way. (My personal favourite from her comments on a recent draft is: 'This is just gobbledygook!') If any of the present text remains 'pompous or unintelligible jargon' then I am to blame, of course, not Ruth. It will simply mean I have not listened to her advice, or have added more gobbledygook in the final re-draft. Even if that has happened, I remain very, very grateful. Her comments have at least made most of the book a much more readable text than it would otherwise have been.

Clive Marsh
September 2005

1 Who is Christ today? Refining Bonhoeffer's challenge

The central question of Christology is this: who is Christ? A sharpened version of it was offered by Dietrich Bonhoeffer from his prison cell in Berlin in 1944, and this has reverberated throughout Christian theology ever since:

> What is bothering me incessantly is the question what Christianity really is, or indeed who Christ really is, for us, today. The time when people could be told everything by means of words, whether theological or pious, is over, and so is the time of inwardness and conscience – and that means the time of religion in general.[1]

There is an urgency in the emphasis on 'today': the past provides no adequate answer to the basic christological question. The 'us' also invites scrutiny. Who is the 'us' today, to whom Christ speaks, and for whom Christ died and lives?

Bonhoeffer was an utterly Christocentric thinker and activist. 'Who is Christ?' was, for him, a life-or-death existential question and the quest for an answer shaped his entire world view and conduct. Looking at the way Bonhoeffer thought about the question can help us to clarify how we should address it today.

'What?', as well as 'who?'

I agree wholeheartedly with Bonhoeffer that Christology must be seen as the heart of Christian thought and practice. However, I differ from him in asking 'what?' Christ is today, as well as 'who?'. As explored in my previous book, *Christ in Focus*, I believe

[1] D. Bonhoeffer, *Letters and Papers from Prison*, London: SCM Press, 1971, p. 279.

that we must recognize Christ today in three interlocking forms. First, Christ is embodied in particular kinds of human relationships – those in which people seek and find justice, worth and dignity. Second, Christ is a spiritual presence within people who seek such relationships. Third, Christ exists as words and images about Jesus/Christ, which are a resource for people in their task of forming justice-seeking relationships. I suggest that Christ exists in all three of these forms simultaneously, and is not reducible to any one of them alone. 'Christ' thus needs to be understood as a fundamentally relational concept, and it is reflection on what Christians have made of Jesus which has enabled this to be seen clearly.

Jesus of Nazareth is a decisive historical figure for Christian faith. He was crucified and, in Christian understanding, is risen and living. However, it is not simply as a past, individual figure that Jesus is proclaimed 'Christ'. A present understanding of Christ therefore informs what is made of the past and vice versa. If the present living form of Jesus as the Christ is that of embodied relationships, then this will be seen reflected in Jesus' own life. And sure enough, Jesus of Nazareth was the Christ in the context of those around him: who followed him, argued with him, misunderstood him, denied him, proclaimed him 'Lord'. In the present, Jesus Christ is encountered among people who suffer, are persecuted, find life, are liberated, experience joy. In short, Christology leaves its task incomplete if it seeks to interpret an isolated, individual figure, especially if that figure is located in the historical past.

Jesus Christ is also best understood relationally because Christ is encountered *among* groups of people who – wittingly or unwittingly, in the context of human life – follow or experience the God who is known as the Father of Jesus Christ. Christology is thus not a task undertaken in the abstract. We can and must interpret who, what and where Christ is today in the context of ordinary, complex human relationships. It is therefore also possible to work back from certain forms of human relationships to what can be said of Christ today.

Sharpening the central question: a conversation with Bonhoeffer

For Bonhoeffer, Christology is the central discipline not simply of the Christian theological task, but of all learning.[2] Further than this, he believes that *the reality of Christ* lies at the heart of Christian thought and practice – a reality that is not to be equated with human ideas or beliefs about Christ. In his exposition of 'the present Christ',[3] Bonhoeffer identifies Christ as word, sacrament and church, central to human existence and history, and at the interface between God and nature. Even the casual reader would be struck by the fact that, for Bonhoeffer, Christocentrism does not therefore mean limiting the centrality of Christ to a centrality *for* the church, or *for* Christian thought and practice. Christ is undoubtedly central to what it means to be church. But in Bonhoeffer's understanding of Christianity 'church' exists for 'world'. In other words, the church exists to serve others, but in serving the world it is not subject to the world's beck and call, or able merely to follow its own chosen path. 'Church' exists for world precisely because it *is* Christ for the world, the form in which Christ is present in the world.

Any exploration of Bonhoeffer's Christocentrism must unpick the close relationship he sees between Christ and church. Does it leave him open to the charge of ecclesiocentrism, despite the safeguards he has built into his approach?[4] Or has Bonhoeffer replaced Christ as centre, not with the church, but with a different form of human community? Is his attempt to locate Christ at the centre of Christian thought and practice therefore ultimately a form of social anthropocentrism?[5] At the very least, what does Bonhoeffer make of the way that Christ relates to, or is evident in, a variety of forms of human community, not only 'church'? Does Bonhoeffer provide significant, positive insights into what form

---

[2] D. Bonhoeffer, *Christology*, London: Fount, 1978, p. 28.
[3] Bonhoeffer, *Christology*, pp. 43–65.
[4] I have considered 'ecclesiocentrism' as one of many possible 'centrisms' that distort Christocentrism in Chapter 3 of *Christ in Focus*.
[5] 'Anthropocentrism' is also one of the 'centrisms' considered in *Christ in Focus* (pp. 53–4).

Christ and Christocentrism take in Christian thought and practice today?

Bonhoeffer's understanding of Jesus/Christ

In his earliest writings, Bonhoeffer explores the interplay of theology, sociology and social philosophy. It is therefore not surprising that his reflections upon the person of Jesus Christ are related directly to understandings of church and human community.[6] I have drawn on both *Sanctorum Communio* and *Act and Being*, as well as sections of Bonhoeffer's later works, *Ethics* and *The Cost of Discipleship*, and shorter writings and letters contained in a variety of collections (not least *Letters and Papers from Prison*).[7] However, Bonhoeffer's most focused writings on Christology are his 1933 lectures, and so these provide the main substance for the following exposition.[8]

Bonhoeffer's most famous formulation of the central christological question, already cited (page 1), is the poignant reiteration of the question which had always preoccupied him in both his academic and his personal life. The 'who?' question about Christ lies at the heart of the 1933 lectures. Rather than become enmeshed in 'how?' questions – for example, how could divine and human natures be united in one person? – Bonhoeffer stresses the need to ask personal questions: about Christ's person

[6] D. Bonhoeffer, *Sanctorum Communio: A Theological Study of the Sociology of the Church*, Minneapolis: Fortress Press, 1998 (written 1925–27; first published Berlin 1930; first ET London: Collins, 1963), *Act and Being*, London: Collins, 1962 (written 1930–31; first published Munich, 1956), his doctorate, and *Habilitationsschrift* (his dissertation written to qualify him to teach), respectively, introduce Bonhoeffer's key theological concerns: revelation, opposition to idealist individualism, church and community, what it means to be human, Christ as key to resolution of individualist tendencies to withdraw from others.

[7] Supplemented by relevant material from D. Bonhoeffer, *No Rusty Swords: Letters, Lectures and Notes 1928–1936*, London: Collins, 1965 and *The Way to Freedom: Letters, Lectures and Notes 1935–1939*, London: Collins, 1966.

[8] The Christology lectures remained incomplete and are reconstructed. (Eberhard Bethge reconstructed the text of the lectures, drawing on notes and recollections of eight students.) Indeed, the third part of the series, 'The Eternal Christ', was probably never delivered. Any attempt to grasp Bonhoeffer's understanding of Christ thus encounters the fragmentary nature of his work. In what follows I interact especially with the two published parts, 'The Present Christ' and 'The Historical Christ', adding to what can be concluded from those sections whatever else can be gleaned from other writings.

and about the enquirer. Who is Christ? Who am I? How are those two questions related?

Christ as 'counter-logos'

Bonhoeffer defines Christ first and foremost as the 'counter-logos'.[9] By this he means that the role of Jesus Christ, as the Word of God, is to correct and redefine any 'word' by which human beings try to describe and order the world in which they live. As counter-logos, Jesus Christ subverts all human attempts to address 'how?' questions in Christology and thus all efforts to include Christ himself within the world of human objects. This means that Jesus Christ has to be understood as an active, living presence, though as the one who confronts us. Christ is not to be claimed or manipulated.

Bonhoeffer seeks to avoid two common ways in which Christology collapses into Jesusology: (1) by referring solely to the individual figure of Jesus of Nazareth;[10] and (2) by overemphasizing the past at cost to the present. The counter-logos is identifiable at a point in history, but is not confined to that point.[11] Indeed, it must not be, as the work of Christ, the counter-logos, continues in the questioning of human beings who seek to find out who they are. This is something that they can only do in relation to Christ.

Christ existing as community

The definition of Christ as 'counter-logos' could suggest that Christ stands over against contemporary experience in an abstract, unrooted, non-material, spiritualized way.[12] Bonhoeffer will have none of this. The phrase that reverberates through much of his work is 'Christ existing as community' (*'Christus als Gemeinde existierend'*).[13] With this expression Bonhoeffer explores

---

[9] Bonhoeffer, *Christology*, p. 30.
[10] On this as a distortion of Christocentrism, see *Christ in Focus*, pp. 44–7.
[11] Bonhoeffer, *Christology*, pp. 30 and 33–4.
[12] To use the threefold categorization of the forms of Christ I used in *Christ is Focus*, this would mean: Christ as 'spiritual presence', though not also as embodied in relationship, and as words and images.
[13] Bonhoeffer, *Sanctorum Communio*, pp. 121, 189–90, 199, 207, 211, 214, 216, 231, 260, 280 and 288; *Act and Being*, pp. 120, 122 and 125.

how Christ is not simply discovered by people in community, but is present as community. He brings 'Christ' and 'church' into the closest proximity. Christ *is* church.

> In and through Christ the church is established in reality. It is not as if Christ could be abstracted from the church; rather it is none other than Christ who 'is' the church . . . Christ did not merely make the church possible, but rather realized it for eternity.[14]

'Christ existing as community' could imply that any collection of human beings, defined in any sense as a 'community', could be deemed to *be* Christ. But this is clearly not Bonhoeffer's view. Christ exists as 'church', but Bonhoeffer knows he needs to be very careful in defining 'church' and in pinpointing where any such 'church' might exist in concrete form.[15] For people assume too easily that they know what 'church' and 'Christ' mean, and so Bonhoeffer must still explain more precisely what 'Christ existing as community' means. He acknowledges the distinction often made between the 'person' and 'work' of Christ.[16] Though he respects both aspects in his exploration, Bonhoeffer's emphasis is clearly on Christ's person. He fears that prioritizing soteriology over Christology, work over person, might run counter to his revelation-based approach to theology. If emphasis is laid on salvation, it is too easy to lose sight of the one saving in favour of the one saved. This danger can be averted by continually asking *who* it is that is doing the saving.

Against this background it is clear that, for Bonhoeffer, 'church' cannot primarily mean a gathering of the redeemed, where the

---

[14] Bonhoeffer, *Sanctorum Communio*, p. 157.

[15] This point relates to the translators' and editor's decision to translate '*Christus als Gemeinde existierend*' as 'Christ existing as church-community' throughout the most recent edition of *Sanctorum Communio* (1998). The editor (Clifford J. Green) rightly stresses (p. 15) that church is defined by where Christ exists as community, and not vice versa. But the inclusion of the word 'church' in the translation does, in my view, have the opposite effect of the intention: i.e., it draws the reader's attention to the church as we know it *first*. The challenge of the interpreter (and then the user) of Bonhoeffer's theology is to grasp the distinctions between the church as we know it, Christ as community, and any human community. Only once these distinctions are allowed their space can Bonhoeffer's challenging concept 'Christ as community' have a chance to work.

[16] Bonhoeffer, *Christology*, pp. 37–9.

emphasis is upon the gathered. Defining Christ as (church-) community in this sense could move the focus away from Christ and onto those incorporated in Christ – that is, those included within this new way of being human in community. The implication might then be that Christ was actually not needed for this human community to exist.

All this does not mean that Bonhoeffer plays down the profoundly personal character of believers' participation in Christ. Near the beginning of the Christology lectures he explores the personal dimension to Christ in relation to those who are Christ's body, the church, and makes the startling statement: 'Every christology which does not begin with the assumption that God is only God for me, Christ is only Christ for me, condemns itself.'[17] This statement might seem to contradict his prioritizing of Christology over soteriology and to turn Bonhoeffer into the existentialist that some have (wrongly) sought to make him.[18] In fact, Bonhoeffer is simply pointing out that detachment from Christ and exploration of Christ's person are incompatible. To be in Christ, one has to be in the church; being in the church (rightly understood) means being in Christ. One cannot be an isolated individual and be 'in Christ'. One must be in a particular form of relationship with others in order to be 'in Christ'. This will then indicate who and what the church is, *in* and *as* Christ.

Bonhoeffer's is thus a Christology of involvement, which also seeks to avoid being a Christology of mere self-assertion, even corporate self-assertion, of those who deem themselves 'saved'. We can only be in Christ, in church, in community, because Christ includes us, and not because we can work towards an understanding of Christ on the basis of our experience of being redeemed.[19]

---

[17] Bonhoeffer, *Christology*, p. 47.

[18] The misleading 'Death of God' appropriation of Bonhoeffer and his work is pertinent here.

[19] It could, I think rightly, be claimed that Bonhoeffer has perhaps gone a bit too far against Melanchthon and his heirs in order to make his point about the *pro me* aspect of Christology and soteriology (Bonhoeffer, *Christology*, pp. 37–9), prior to making his more positive point (p. 47). But this is not a matter that needs discussing here.

Christ as Word

Bonhoeffer takes two steps to explain further what 'Christ existing as community' means. Though he introduced his understanding of Christ and community in his first two works, the
exposition of 'the present Christ' in the 1933 lectures prefaces
exploration of Christ as community with expositions of Christ as
'word' and Christ as 'sacrament'.[20] In the same way that
Bonhoeffer redefines 'church', it is no surprise to find him taking
the two necessary steps to redefine 'word' and 'sacrament' too,
lest anyone assumes that they understand what these are and
believes that they have grasped in advance the form of Christ's
presence.

Again, Bonhoeffer works with a corporate understanding of
Christ. Resisting a notion of a timeless word or a disembodied
idea,[21] Bonhoeffer sees Christ in terms of concrete address to the
human person, in the context of an addressed community.

> The character of truth in this addressing word is such that it
> seeks community, in order to face it with the truth. Truth is
> not something in itself, which rests for itself, but something
> that happens between two. Truth happens only in commu-
> nity. It is here for the first time that the concept of the Word
> acquires its full significance.[22]

Bonhoeffer has already expressed his agreement with Martin
Kähler a few pages beforehand: 'The Christ who is preached is
the real Christ.'[23] Here we see how important it is for Bonhoeffer
that Christ is preached in the context of the community of Christ
(for the community, rightly understood, is Christ present). As the
Word, Christ is not preached in a detached way, as if the Word is
but words:

[20] Bonhoeffer, *Christology*, pp. 49–58.
[21] And here Bonhoeffer sounds like Bultmann, though without displaying
Bultmann's individualist tendencies.
[22] Bonhoeffer, *Christology*, p. 50.
[23] Bonhoeffer, *Christology*, p. 46, echoing M. Kähler, *The So-Called Historical Jesus and
the Historic Biblical Christ*, Philadelphia: Fortress Press, 1964 (German original,
1892), p. 71. The debt is acknowledged later in the Christology lectures in the
context of Bonhoeffer's discussion of the 'Historical Christ' (Bonhoeffer,
Christology, p. 70).

Christ is not only present *in* the Word of the Church, but also *as* Word of the Church, that means the spoken Word of preaching. *In* the Word, could be too little, because it could separate Christ from his Word.[24]

Again the insistence on the concrete, communal embodiment of Christ is evident. Christ is not to become an idea, or even simply a sermon, despite the crucial significance of preaching.[25] Christ as word and Christ as community belong together, in so far as the preaching addresses the recipient within the context of the real, concrete human relationships which 'church' makes possible.

Christ as sacrament

'Word' clearly has priority over sacrament in Bonhoeffer's interpretation of Christ. Recognizing Christ to be 'Word' secures the revelation-based, God-centredness of Christ and of any understanding of Christ.[26] But given the nature of Bonhoeffer's attention to 'Christ existing as community', it is inevitable that Bonhoeffer feels pressed to say more about the form of Christ's concrete presence. 'Word' could still remain too immaterial. As 'sacrament' Christ is present as 'embodied Word'.[27] The gospel is proclaimed as clearly via a sacrament – water, or bread and wine – as via the word of preaching. Here we see God making use of fallible created material: 'against the attempt to limit Christ to doctrine, or to lose him in general truth, the Church stresses the sacramental form of Christ. He is not only doctrine, nor only idea, but nature and history.'[28]

The concreteness of the church is thus directly reflected in the concrete form of the word as sacrament. The 'God-Human Being' is present in tangible form in the present, despite 'the inadequa-

---

[24] Bonhoeffer, *Christology*, p. 51 (Bonhoeffer's emphasis).

[25] 'If the complete Christ is not in the preaching, then the Church is broken' (Bonhoeffer, *Christology*, p. 52).

[26] It is worth noting that Bonhoeffer, in rather stereotypical Protestant fashion (and despite his love of music), has just excluded other possibilities prior to developing this second form of Christ's presence in his discussion: 'Christ is present in the church as the spoken word, not as music nor as art' (Bonhoeffer, *Christology*, p. 52).

[27] Bonhoeffer, *Christology*, p. 53.

[28] Bonhoeffer, *Christology*, pp. 53–4.

cies of nature and history'. Though the material forms of Christ's presence as water, bread or wine may be termed 'God's cloak', they do not lead to God's devaluing of the material world as a whole. For as God is revealed in the flesh of Jesus, so also Christ is revealed in the sacrament of bread and wine 'not as straw is in a sack; this *in* must be understood theologically'.[29]

Consistent with his whole approach to Christology, Bonhoeffer again resists venturing too far into the question of 'how' Christ is present. He takes up the topic with great reluctance, and with astonishing brevity given how much attention has been paid to it throughout Christian history.

> '*Who* is present *in the sacrament*?', is the only question to ask. The complete person of the God-Man is present, in his exaltation and humiliation' is the answer. Christ exists in such a way that he is existentially present in the sacrament. His being in the sacrament is not a special property, one quality among others; this is the way in which he exists in the Church. The humiliation is no accident of his divine-human substance, but it is his existence.[30]

Bonhoeffer in effect invites us to consider Christ as a community of three circles in which the outer circle is the community in which Christ is manifest, an inner circle the sacramental form of Christ and the innermost circle Christ as word. All of these together constitute the communal form which Christ strives to take in the world. In this way, Bonhoeffer preserves the priority of revelation (as word), and remains fully concrete and communal in his Christocentrism.

Jesus Christ as word, sacrament and church: a summary

Human life is to be interpreted, for Bonhoeffer, through these three lenses. Christ is community, but is identifiable neither with the church as we know it nor merely any form of community.

---

[29] Bonhoeffer, *Christology*, p. 56, where Bonhoeffer is following Luther; the nature of the presence of Christ 'in' the water of baptism has, of course, been explored less and is, not surprisingly, not a question raised by Bonhoeffer.

[30] Bonhoeffer, *Christology*, p. 57.

Christ is community when read in the light of word and sacrament. Not everything is sacramental. Word and sacrament disclose where true church 'is' and thus where Christ is. Word and sacrament are not dispensable media, as if some disembodied 'Christ' could be evident behind or beyond them. Word, sacrament and church belong together.[31]

We must now go on to ask, however, whether the potential for Bonhoeffer's approach radically to critique a customary understanding of 'church' is not undermined by the manner of his attention to word and sacrament.

Jesus/Christ in Bonhoeffer's theology: a critical analysis

Christ and otherness

The first critical question to pose to Bonhoeffer concerns whether he as consistently holds to the identification of Christ as (church-) community as his work implies. Bonhoeffer notes in his discussion of Paul's exploration of Christ and the church that a 'complete identification between Christ and the church-community cannot be made'.[32] He is, however, insistent on attention to the revelation of God in Christ in this life and in the present time. This latter emphasis is linked with Bonhoeffer's opposition to all forms of idealism, or monism of the spirit, which in his view places too much store by the individual detached from the concrete demands of actual living.[33] But has Bonhoeffer carried through this opposition consistently? It seems to me that Bonhoeffer's recognition that a Christ/community equation is not made by Paul is both a helpful challenge to the tenor of Bonhoeffer's thought and a necessary reminder of how a complete opposition to idealism in all its forms is simply not possible in Christianity.

---

[31] At this point it is worth noting that there is a correlation, even if not a perfect one, between Bonhoeffer's conclusions and those to which I came at the end of *Christ in Focus*. 'Church' relates to embodied relationships, 'sacrament' relates to relationships and to 'words and images', and 'Word' relates to words and images and spiritual presence. The value of my different construal, I suggest, lies in its movement beyond overly ecclesiastical categories.

[32] Bonhoeffer, *Sanctorum Communio*, p. 140.

[33] Bonhoeffer, *Sanctorum Communio*, pp. 160–1.

It is clear why Bonhoeffer feels unable wholly to equate Christ with any communal form: to do so risks confusing creator with creature, God with (fallible) humanity.[34] Such an approach would fall into the trap of working from contemporary experience back to the reality of God (rather than vice versa). The liberals of Bonhoeffer's time, whom Bonhoeffer opposed, were not all guilty of this,[35] but such a theological procedure could undoubtedly play into the hands of the German Christians in their preoccupation with 'relevance' and their desire to justify Christianity in terms of the present.[36] In order to avoid the trap, Bonhoeffer stresses the primacy of revelation, and thus the independent, free action of God. But he must do this, it seems to me, in a way which requires him to make some use of idealism. The ontology that Bonhoeffer needs to support his own emphasis on 'Christ as community' is not without its own idealist strain. There is always an 'otherness' needed outside of the concrete form in which Christ is present to enable the claim to be made that it is *Christ* who is present. In other words, Bonhoeffer supports an implicit ontology of a form which subverts the ontology he supports in *Act and Being*. He remains more idealist than he thinks he is, wants to be, and believes is good for Christian theology.

Idealism need not be characterized in the devilish terms which Bonhoeffer implies. A recognition of the importance of the non-material aspects of human living does not inevitably lead to Nazism. Bonhoeffer's trenchant critique of much German Christianity in the 1930s and 1940s was admittedly necessary given the tendency to favour an eternal, timeless, ethereal Christ. Bonhoeffer saw such an ideological commitment to be inadequate. For him, Christ must always be 'other' (as the 'counter-logos') but always also concrete and corporate. It is, as we see here, in the conceptuality of maintaining that sense of otherness that difficulties arise.

How, then, is the otherness of God in Christ to be respected? One may accept that identifying Christ with community need not be quite as negative towards idealism as Bonhoeffer makes out.

---

[34] Something which, in 1930s Germany, Bonhoeffer saw to be dangerous.

[35] As Bonhoeffer recognizes (and here he is more charitable than Barth), *No Rusty Swords*, p. 309.

[36] Bonhoeffer, *No Rusty Swords*, p. 310.

But how could Bonhoeffer be reassured that a human community claiming to embody Christ does so in a valid way? Bonhoeffer himself makes use of a christological criterion in order to determine the true from the false church (the church is wherever Christ takes shape). But how is such a christological criterion to operate? In order to be able to present Christ as existing as community without inevitably collapsing Christ into community without remainder, there at least needs to be a *narrative tradition* about (the) Christ, in relation to which claims of Christ's communal presence can be cross-checked.[37] Christ cannot be identified in, with or as a community, without a means through which a community can be thus identified. Recognizing that 'Christ' is words and images as well as being a spiritual presence and embodied in relationships offers a broad channel through which the presence of Christ can be identified. The ways in which people fashion images of Jesus in the Christian tradition is a prime means through which God-talk is undertaken. The fact that this happens as *images* as well as words challenges and extends Bonhoeffer's reluctance to attach equal significance to the visual as well as the verbal. The importance and sheer difficulty of critically assessing the many and varied words and images that present Christ remains. But the necessity, the value and the practical function of such images is clear. They are the way in which God in Christ is not collapsed wholly into the concrete forms in which Christ is nevertheless seen to be present. They are a link between the concrete form of Christ and the otherness of the God revealed.

Relating in Christ

A second question to ask in studying Bonhoeffer's work is whether he sufficiently explores the nature of the relationships

---

[37] There will doubtless need to be much more. For Bonhoeffer himself this narrative tradition is biblical. Biblical material will inevitably feature prominently in any such Christian argumentation. To what extent the Bible might be supplemented by other sources, however normatively it might function, is an important question. I am thus using 'narrative' in a broad sense here. The recognition of Christ existing as 'words and images' and as 'spiritual presence' (see *Christ in Focus*) is important here. A link can also be made with my suggestion that Rita Nakashima Brock underestimates the extent to which she needs a 'narrative Jesus' in her Christology (*Christ in Focus*, Ch. 6).

between people within the community/communities that Christ can be held to 'exist as'. In some ways, Bonhoeffer offers a simple answer: Christ exists only as *church*-community. So my question is posed only in regard to his definition and exploration of 'church', and a direct response comes from his exposition of life at the community he formed in Finkenwalde.[38] Christ creates the sense of Christians belonging to one another,[39] and any sense of mutual belonging derives solely from Christ.[40] It is thus from 'church' that we understand what 'community' (and human relationship) is. It is in the light of the existence of Christian community that we can grasp what human community might be. Without a sense of Christian community, we do not, in Bonhoeffer's view, understand what it is possible for human community to be.

Yet things are not as simple as this, and the degree to which Bonhoeffer plays off 'church' against 'world' (even if understandable in his historical context) leaves ill explored the nature of relationships within 'church' as he defines it. If we are to place Christ centrally in Christian thought and practice, and if Christ is to be grasped as a corporate concept, then the actual nature of the relationships between those who constitute the corporateness of Christ must be examined. If Christ is relational, what kind of relationships are to be fostered? Standing in relationship with others does not necessarily mean that one enjoys good, life-enhancing, empowering relationships.[41]

Bonhoeffer's insights in this regard can be teased out further from his *Ethics*, but a full discussion of this cannot be entered into here.[42] Suffice it to say that while much fruitful exploration of Christian conduct and relationships (inside and outside of the faith community) can be developed from Bonhoeffer's reflections on the self-expenditure of the Christian 'for others', the particular

---

[38] D. Bonhoeffer, *Life Together*, London: SCM Press, 1954.

[39] Bonhoeffer, *Life Together*, p. 10.

[40] Bonhoeffer, *Life Together*, p. 14.

[41] Though it is worth noting how easily in current theological discussion 'relationality', 'relation' or 'relationship' are seen as positive words.

[42] L. Rasmussen's essay, 'The ethics of responsible action' in J. De Gruchy (ed.), *The Cambridge Companion to Dietrich Bonhoeffer*, Cambridge: Cambridge University Press, 1999, pp. 206–25; and many of the essays in J. De Gruchy (ed.), *Bonhoeffer for a New Day*, Grand Rapids: Eerdmans, 1997, are useful starting points.

way in which he makes use of the 'church/world' framework does tend to leave the 'church' framework itself underdeveloped as a model of social practice. Further, Bonhoeffer terms as 'mandates' a number of forms of social living which in his view require closest scrutiny (labour, marriage, government and church).[43] He also refers to friendship, art, education and play as 'spheres of freedom'.[44] However, there is a relative lack of critique of these social frameworks and practices within which an encounter with Christ can occur. It could be argued that both the mandates and the 'spheres of freedom' could be used in the service of developing a more comprehensive relational Christology. The 'church/world' distinction, as Bonhoeffer interprets it within his own time, makes it impossible to reach a fuller corporate understanding of Christ; one which does justice to the fact that most of human living is not, in fact, lived as 'church'.

Christian thought and practice after Bonhoeffer is therefore left the task of identifying what form such an undertaking might take, without reducing Christology to ethics or to mere 'application' of a definition of Christ worked out beforehand. Discovering who Christ is will always in part be the result of participation in the social forms in which Christ is present in the world today.

Bonhoeffer's 'church optimism'

As a response to the question about the relational character of his Christology, Bonhoeffer's reference to 'church' could well seem inadequate. By 'church', of course, he did not mean the church in any simple form as concretely evident (not 'the religious community' as such). He could only actually be pro-church in a limited way, given the concrete setting in which he worked out his (christological) criterion for identifying what 'church' should be. Even so, his approach remains too subtle and his use of 'church' as a

---

[43] D. Bonhoeffer, *Ethics*, London: SCM Press, 1955, pp. 73–8. On the concept of 'mandate', see especially *Ethics*, pp. 254–8. Three mandates are listed in Bonhoeffer, *Letters and Papers*, pp. 192–3 (family, society and work). Bonhoeffer comes closest to anticipating what I am attempting to do in this book in *Ethics*, pp. 264–7. Even here, however, the actual detail of what this means for daily living is insufficiently explored.

[44] Bonhoeffer, *Letters and Papers*, p. 193.

category surprisingly optimistic. Even if what 'church' is can only be seen on the basis of revelation,[45] and even if all concrete manifestations of 'church' are recognized as imperfect, communal living with God is certainly, for Bonhoeffer, 'church-dependent'. It is, though, understandable if one's focus then falls on the forms of church that we actually know, even if this is the wrong way round: the concrete form of church then defining who and what Christ is rather than vice versa.

It is therefore difficult to put Bonhoeffer's insights fully to work outside of their immediate context. His critique of concrete manifestations of 'church' can be put to good use. At the opposite pole, his opposition to the view that the church somehow 'exists' as an idea outside of time remains important. But it is very clear that further exploration is needed of the forms of human relationships that would not readily be defined as 'church', yet which may correlate with forms of human community worthy of linking with Jesus/Christ.[46] The surprising optimism of Bonhoeffer's understanding of church – an 'optimism' born only of God, as working in and through Christ and the Spirit – leaves little, if any, room for the positive interpretation of forms of human community outside of identifiable Christianity. Even in Christian terms I am not sure that Bonhoeffer quite leaves as much room as he supposes for the appreciation of the mandates as forms in which Christ can be present in the world. All four mandates are to be christologically understood ('each in its own way, shall be through Christ, directed towards Christ, and in Christ').[47] But the divine mandate of church is clearly of a different order from the other three, despite the fact that Christians live in the world, in relation to all three other mandates, like anyone else.[48] In remaining, despite his best insights, strangely optimistic about 'church', Bonhoeffer was certainly a man of his time, and of his culture. More than fifty years on, a different approach must be adopted in exploring the

---

[45] Bonhoeffer, *Sanctorum Communio*, p. 134.

[46] This point is already to assume the direction of much later discussion, but seems necessary at this stage. The point may be formulated as a question: does every form of human relationality that Christians may identify as 'Christ existing as community' need also to be identified as 'church'?

[47] Bonhoeffer, *Ethics*, p. 73.

[48] Bonhoeffer, *Ethics*, p. 76.

relationality claimed for the corporate forms in which Christ is seen to take form in the world.

These are, then, three critical questions which may be brought to Bonhoeffer's Christology:

• How can Christ remain 'other' when emphasis is so firmly placed on Christ's concrete presence as community?
• What kind of relationships are we talking about here?
• Is not Bonhoeffer over-optimistic about what we can glean about Christ in and through 'church'?

There is no way in which these critical observations prevent Bonhoeffer's insights being of profound usefulness for our own enquiry. But they are worth noting because they alert us to some of the pitfalls of trying to identify who and where Christ is for us today.

Bonhoeffer's practical challenge

A crucial, positive point emerges from this discussion of Bonhoeffer. His 'theological study of the sociology of the church', in *Sanctorum Communio*, provides both a christological reading of the church and a corporate Christology. 'Church' cannot be understood appropriately except as a concrete manifestation of the living Christ. Christ cannot be experienced except from within the context of corporate human experience. These assertions challenge all ensuing Christian theologies to clarify whether they relate 'Christ' and 'church', to what extent they do this, and how they understand the relationship between individual and corporate Christian existence. Any attempt to define Christ or church without reference to concrete human experience becomes questionable. At the same time, Bonhoeffer's method rules out lazy extrapolations from human experience – be it individual or corporate. Bonhoeffer wishes all the time to find ways of ensuring that, in theology, we speak about *God*, rather than merely human ideas about God, or about human experience (religious or otherwise).[49]

---

[49] We must, in fact, say that humans only 'have' experience at all because God is.

His achievement is to stress that the God we know in Christ becomes known in corporate human experience of a certain kind (which can be called 'church'). Experience of God, we might say, is received as a gift in the midst of human relationships of a particular nature and quality. Such corporate experience, which we may term 'redeemed sociality' in so far as it is a form of communal living that God intends for creation,[50] may indeed only be identifiable because of 'church'.[51] But it is not clear that it is either logical or Christian to claim that all examples of such 'redeemed sociality' should be labelled 'church'.[52] Indeed, as Daniel Hardy notes, the insights that the apostle Paul offered in the context of early Christianity concerned the 'discovery of the presence of the risen Christ in the world itself'. Paul's experience was 'a constant finding of Christ'.[53]

To Paul's insight we might well add, with Bonhoeffer, that the development and enjoyment of relationships of a quality worth describing as just, redeemed and redemptive, forgiving, inspiring

---

[50] A phrase I first encountered in D. W. Hardy, 'Created and Redeemed Sociality' in C. Gunton and D. W. Hardy (eds), *On Being the Church: Essays on the Christian Community*, Edinburgh: T & T Clark, 1989, pp. 21–47 (reprinted in D. W. Hardy, *God's Ways with the World: Thinking and Practising Christian Faith*, Edinburgh: T & T Clark, 1996, pp. 188–205).

[51] In the sense that Christians will only be able to identify particular human communities as examples of such 'redeemed sociality' because of the church's carrying with it the traditions about God in Christ which enable such perceptions. It may even be claimed that humanity in general may depend upon Christian communities for the same.

[52] An ascription that may, of course, be most unwelcome to some groups! Whether or not this would be an appropriate move, or an adequate theology of inclusivism, cannot be gone into here. Suffice it to say: to make such a move is of primary concern to the Christians who make it. To discuss what benefit would be gained by groups so described is another matter.

[53] Hardy, 'Created and Redeemed Sociality', p. 205. I note in passing here, without underplaying the potential significance of the point, that Hardy distinguishes the notion of 'social transcendental' from 'idealism' in this essay, wanting to hold to the former without committing himself to the latter. Hardy is supportive of Bonhoeffer's critique of idealism, though not of his suspicion about transcendentals. I must admit that I am unsure that the distinctions being drawn here carry much weight in practice. For my purpose, I want to hold to the notion that no person simply 'is' in oneself. We are because of an Other (God) and discover this through others (people). But we also need a conceptual or narrative framework through which we can grasp this. These frameworks are linguistic attempts to acknowledge that God (who 'is' independently of us) is nevertheless fundamentally relational and committed to self-expenditure to enable creation to be, to be redeemed, and to struggle towards completion.

and empowering, will, in Christian understanding, always be made with reference to Christ. But Bonhoeffer's approach appears to do two things: it assumes that Christianity has a monopoly upon the promotion of such relationships; and it so centralizes the role of 'church' that Bonhoeffer cannot escape the charge of ecclesiocentrism.[54] There seems simply no room for any group outside of Christianity to discover what it means to be forgiven, redeemed or empowered – even if Christians may then attribute the emergence of such redemption to God, acting in Christ. Perhaps that is precisely Bonhoeffer's point: it cannot happen. Christocentrism means *solus Christus*. Because redemption, forgiveness or empowerment happen 'by Christ alone', they can only happen *consciously* 'by Christ alone'. Without such consciousness, we are back in the realm of human self-assertion, and any group might make the claim to be 'redeemed' (or offer some equivalent concept or experience).[55]

Bonhoeffer does not overlook the need to ask what *kind* of relationships are being fostered when any community is claimed to be redemptive and empowering. But he does not make clear how, by means of a christological criterion, it can be judged, say, that a National Socialist group could make no legitimate claim to embody Christ, in contrast to a community of Sikhs living in a Christ-like way.[56] At this point, then, we can begin to appreciate the full force of the question posed about the relational aspects of Bonhoeffer's corporate Christology. It is not enough to relate 'Christ' closely either with 'church' or indeed with any notion of human community. 'Christ' has to inform an understanding of the kinds of relationships that people work at and seek to form within the context of everyday patterns of life. What this all means for a contemporary practical Christology forms the substance of the rest of this book.

Not only must Christian theology be Christocentric, Christian living must be too. Such living cannot be abstract or individualis-

---

[54] Even allowing for Bonhoeffer's bold attempt to redefine church through Christ.
[55] And then the door is open for National Socialists to make a claim to be 'saving' the German people.
[56] It is intriguing to ask how Bonhoeffer would have responded to the notion that a family in the Nazi era (who, say, hid Jews on the run, yet whose sons were in the Hitler youth) might be embodying Christ while not necessarily claiming Christian allegiance.

tic. It is crucial to clarify the social forms of Christ, and thus how the presence of Christ both informs and actively shapes human living. 'Church' cannot be ignored. There is no Christian living without reference to, and participation in, 'church' of some kind. But as the critical discussion of his work has highlighted, Bonhoeffer failed to explore adequately the multiple social forms in which Christ may be present in the world. While identifying the practical theological significance of 'church', Bonhoeffer has not gone far enough beyond the social form of 'church' in seeking to clarify how and where Christ is in the world today. Though not writing with Bonhoeffer in view, Rowan Williams' comment is pertinent.

> Family and nation, in particular, are of themselves good patterns of sociality, needing only the context of incarnational theology to save them from idolatry and set them on a firm base. But the secular analyst of ideology may object: if you say that the social forms of family and nation are good, but waiting for the seal of Christian completion, precisely *what* forms are you talking about?[57]

Family and nation (and work) are, as Williams recognizes, all liable to idolization. They are not ends in themselves. The firm base on which they can be set is not, however, by being more like church or even being related to church (however understood). They deserve christological interpretation so that what they are capable of being in their own right, and the people they are capable of forming, better befit the work of the God who creates, redeems and sanctifies.

This present book works in the light of the recognition that Christ takes form in the world as 'church'. But it pushes further. It asks what it means to speak of a 'Christology of everyday life'. It does not label relationships as 'Christ' because they are vaguely 'good', 'useful' or 'helpful'. It recognizes that to speak of Christ taking social form entails analysing the accepted and institutional forms of social and political life beyond church: family, friendships, work relationships, educational life, nation state. It seeks not to be a book of 'applied theology'. Aspects of who Christ is

---

[57] R. Williams, 'Incarnation and the Renewal of Community' in *On Christian Theology*, Oxford and Malden: Blackwell, 2000, p. 228.

are not merely *confirmed* through critical, christological analysis of the different social forms; they are *discovered*. We learn more about who Christ is by being friends, by being children and parents, and by engaging in the complexity of employment relationships. I suggest that such an approach is wholly in keeping with Bonhoeffer's intention, and this is why discussion of his work has been a good place to start. We can now go on to press the question 'who is Christ for us today?' by asking: what is Christ doing in the midst of national, family, working and educational life, and among friends, as well as in the form of church?

2 Where in the world is Christ today? Christology as ethical challenge

The aim of this chapter is to identify christological patterns in human life. We need to locate the traces of the presence of Christ we should expect to find, before we go on, in later chapters, to explore institutional forms of living as contexts in which Christ may be deemed to be present. What will Christ 'look like' in the midst of human life today? How will we recognize Christ? In what circumstances should we expect to find Christ?

Such an enquiry is an ethical as well as a theological challenge. Who people believe God to be affects behaviour, and vice versa. Traces of Christ's presence are therefore bound up with what people do as well as what people think and believe. This means that locating Christ is as much about identifying patterns of action as about words of confession. We do, though, need to have some sense in advance of who Christ is, otherwise we would not be able to put a name to the face we see. Christian traditions about Christ (in words and images) enable us to do this.[1] Narratives (gospels), icons, creeds, confessions, plays, sculptures, paintings and much else besides create a working image, as a result of which it becomes possible to say 'there is Christ'. Christian tradition supplies a range of images – a vulnerable baby, an activist preacher of the reign of God, a healer and miracle-worker, and a crucified and risen figure – as lenses through which contemporary life can be viewed. Stories and pictures of Jesus' life enable us to locate God in the circumstances of human life in any age. The fact that particular ways of human behaving can be linked to the stories and pictures of Jesus that the Christian tradition carries demonstrates what incarnation

[1] Christ in the form of 'words and images' (on which, see *Christ in Focus*, pp. 177–86).

means. God is the sort of God who is revealed in the midst of human interaction. Because of this, it is possible to speak of this God, and identify where this God is at work, in the form of the story of a human life. God's activity is by no means confined to the lifespan of Jesus of Nazareth: far from it. But God's continued working is consistent with that life, especially in the social settings in which he operated and the movement he initiated. God also continues to work with the groups and communities that stand in continuity with Jesus and his followers by seeking to act like them.

The theological task of locating God's presence and activity in the world through reference to the story of Jesus Christ works best when it includes a thorough knowledge of the narratives and images within which human life is to be interpreted.[2] As a collection of narratives, images and many other forms of communication, 'Christian tradition' is ultimately not reducible to a set of doctrinal formulae, however necessary it may be to patrol the borders of what constitutes Christian belief. Nevertheless, it is important to highlight certain key motifs from the Jesus tradition, for it is such motifs that enable us to detect God's presence. The God who is Christ-like is discernible because the shapes of human living present in the story of Jesus Christ are repeated, and are recognizable, in contemporary life.[3]

Identifying the presence of God in Christ: an approach through motifs from the story of Jesus

One of the most common ways of offering theological interpretations of works of literature or film is to identify 'Christ-figures'.[4]

---

[2] By 'knowledge' here I do not simply mean 'knowing about', though it includes that. Knowledge of the Jesus narratives, at its best, means 'working with' and 'seeking to live within'. The Gospels are, as John Dominic Crossan has rightly noted, texts that demand performance.

[3] The notion of 'shapes' or 'patterns' is insightfully used by Peter Hodgson in *Winds of the Spirit*, London: SCM Press, 1994, pp. 250–64. Though I use the image somewhat differently here, I am nevertheless grateful for the stimulus provided by Hodgson's work.

[4] Among many such treatments, see e.g. T. Ziolkowski, *Fictional Transfigurations of Jesus*, Princeton: Princeton University Press, 1972, and C. Deacy, *Screen Christologies: Redemption and the Medium of Film*, Cardiff: University of Wales Press, 2001.

This is an understandable approach. Identifying a character who behaves like the figure of Jesus from the canonical Gospels seems to be a means of teasing out meaning from a story. Whether or not a writer or film-maker intended it, if a link between a character and the figure of Jesus seems plausible, then a christological interpretation can be offered.

The approach to be adopted here does not rely on such individualism. In my view, Christology has become too fixated on the individual Jesus in isolation, at cost to understanding what it means to follow Jesus in a communal context. The main purpose of my previous book, *Christ in Focus*, was to demonstrate this, and so I can hardly now resort to looking for individuals who resemble the figure of Jesus in some way! Indeed, searching for such individuals would merely reduce the capacity of the story of Jesus Christ to be a means of locating the presence and activity of God in the world. Thinking of God's presence and activity in Christ in terms of 'shapes' or 'patterns' of living makes it possible to look at human life more broadly and imaginatively. The challenge is of considerable ethical import, as will become clear, for the shapes and patterns of living which the story of Jesus Christ invites us to consider can draw attention to things we might wish to overlook. It is not possible to carry a tradition about a crucified figure and then expect to be able to see God at work only and always in positive, transformative ways. God's work of creation and redemption remains ongoing. The world is still an incomplete divine project. Resurrection and the reign of God have been anticipated and are only partly here.

How, then, can we detect the presence and activity of God as known in Christ today? What motifs from the story of Jesus Christ should we be looking for? An overarching one is that of *loving relationships which enable people to flourish as human beings*. If God is love, then the created order is a context in which God is at work to enable God's creatures to be free to flourish. Though true, such a statement about being 'free to flourish' may sound too vague to be of much use in practice. It needs spelling out in more concrete terms (the task of this chapter) and then rooting further in the actual complex structures of everyday living (Chapters 3 to 6). For it is such rooting which reminds us that creatureliness (the fact that being human is a created, dependent state) brings constraints. Human flourishing simply does not occur evenly and easily throughout the created order. No one is wholly free, and all are not equally free. The freedom to flourish is bound by the constraints that are inevitable in a created order which is 'allowed to be', and where freedoms therefore conflict.

It is easy to look at the canonical Gospels and conclude that where 'the blind receive their sight, the lame walk, the lepers are cleansed, the deaf hear, the dead are raised, and the poor have good news brought to them' (Matt. 11.5), then God in Christ is clearly at work. Such occurrences clearly function as examples of human flourishing. Furthermore, they are examples of embodied flourishing and cannot all be reduced to metaphors for inner spiritual change. The 'raising of the dead' must admittedly be understood metaphorically, and we do not know the extent to which Jesus' miracles were actual changes of physical state. But we can be sure that the action and impact of Jesus upon people did change their circumstances (in some cases, materially – being fed, for example) and that the end of their social exclusion meant a new form of existence. Despite this, more needs to be said both about what such transformation in relation to Jesus Christ amounts to and about the realism of any contemporary echoes of what the Gospels describe.

What, then, can be said in more detail from the accounts in the Gospels, when brought alongside contemporary experience? What follows is an exploration of aspects of human living which are central to the gospel narratives. What prevents their being merely a list of laudable human actions is that their understanding and interpretation is informed throughout by a Christocentric theology, articulated in the form of Jesus narratives.[5]

Wherever people suffer innocently or for a just cause

God in Christ is the companion of anyone who suffers, however their suffering has come about. But suffering is not willed as part

---

[5] This list is not meant to be exhaustive. I regard these as some of the key features of the story pertinent to the enquiry of the social forms of Christ in the chapters to follow. The motifs draw on, and extend in a practical direction, the eight subsections of Chapter 8 in *Christ in Focus*.

of Christian practice. Jesus of Nazareth anticipated that his words and actions were likely to bring him into conflict with those who had political power over him and could do him harm (Mark 8.31; 9.31; 10.33); and he expected that those who followed after him would suffer likewise (Mark 8.34–38). Yet expecting suffering in this way is quite different from approaching life desiring suffering. Christianity is not a form of masochism. It is a way of life which acknowledges without flinching the way the world is, and invites people to connect with its insights and practices, thereby relating to the God of Jesus Christ. This means that, where suffering occurs, people do not sidestep or deny it. They face suffering and, where possible, overcome it.[6]

Recognizing that God was with Jesus in the midst of the most intense experience of suffering means that Christian faith recognizes the presence and activity of God wherever innocent suffering or suffering for a just cause occurs. Many examples can be cited. Those who mourn suffer unjustly, and yet will be comforted (Matt. 5.4). Those who suffer as a result of seeking justice (Matt. 5.6, 10) – be it with respect to employment rights, fair trade, or the right to vote – defend causes which are bound up with human flourishing. Those who suffer within families as a result of protecting children or siblings from abusive parents are 'where Christ is' today.

In none of these cases is the suffering acceptable. In no case is it of itself 'redemptive'. Easy acceptance of suffering – as if recognition of its apparent inevitability amounts to putting up with it as acceptable – has led to misreadings and misuse of doctrines of atonement and to the frequent failure on the part of Christians to oppose injustice or abuse. On the grounds that 'God is with us, in Christ, in the midst of abuse' or that suffering will be overcome 'some day' in 'the hereafter', it has often simply been endured. Diseases and physical violence alike have to be opposed. But they are different enemies and require different strategies of opposition. Medical and pastoral care and inner strength, applicable in

---

[6] The clause 'where possible' relates precisely to contemporary reception of the gospel stories. Were lepers always healed of their leprosy? Were some of the cases not leprosy but a wide range of diseases which rendered their sufferers social outcasts, and it was the overcoming of their social ostracism which Jesus brought about? In other words: even God may not be in a position to rid all suffering. But God in Christ is present to face all suffering, to be active in getting rid of it when possible, or enabling people to live with it when necessary.

the former case, are inadequate by themselves in the latter, where physical removal and protection may also be needed.

One other observation about suffering is crucial. In the comfortable West it is too easy to be glib about suffering and to lose perspective. All suffering is awful, and it is invidious to grade cases of suffering.[7] But a loss of perspective can enter into many contemporary discussions about 'fighting for a cause' when, for example, at issue is the number of places available at schools with small percentage differences in examination performances. It is legitimate to ask whether God in Christ is active and present with parents who claim to 'suffer for a just cause', when what may be at stake is the cause only of their own children.[8] Likewise, in higher education, I have experienced dramatic use of language in the midst of managerial conflicts ('only we were prepared to put our heads above the parapet'). There is little doubt that the sense of injustice in such conflicts is real, and the cause may well be deemed just. However, definitions of what constitutes a 'just cause' can become stretched. In academic life, for example, the maintenance of 'academic freedom', that is, a job flexibility which many others may not be privileged to enjoy, or to job continuation for pension purposes alone may be at stake. These are not small matters. But they are the concerns of the already wealthy.

Reading contemporary experience of suffering through the insights of the Gospels can, then, provide a healthy and sobering perspective on what is meant by suffering and what constitutes a 'just cause'.

When solidarity is shown with those who are mistreated

When any attempt is made to live in the light of the stories of Jesus as found in the Gospels, then it is not only with the suffering of

---

[7] Though, of course, as those in the medical profession are aware, this has to be done, especially in a crisis situation. Triage is precisely this: assessing the urgent from the less urgent cases.

[8] Such glib use of language is neatly satirized in the film *Notting Hill*, when Spike (Rhys Ifans) responds to William's (Hugh Grant) reference to losing his glasses as 'one of life's real cruelties' with the words 'That's compared to, like, earthquakes in the Far East or testicular cancer?' (R. Curtis, *Notting Hill*, London: Hodder & Stoughton, 1999, p. 78).

Jesus that a contemporary person may identify. Those who consciously follow Jesus are invited to take up the cross (Mark 8.34–35). In Mark, these words are addressed to the crowd, not just the disciples (as is the case in Matt. 16). The implication in Mark is that you become a disciple by showing your willingness to take up the cross. Mark's Gospel, while a manifesto for disciples, is also a summons to readers and hearers to take the risk of being a disciple.

Again, this is not the way of masochism. It is simply a case of accepting that people who stand in solidarity with those who are mistreated may themselves be mistreated too. Detecting how God in Christ is present and active in the world, and seeking to participate in that action 'in Christ', will not be an easy way of trying to be human. But in Christian understanding it is the only way to be fully human.

As already noted, those whom Jesus heals in the gospel stories are released as much from their social exclusion as from their physical ailments. So Jesus not only healed but befriended people he knew were unpopular, or were excluded from normal human relations (Mark 2.15–17). Companionship with those who are mistreated in any way is ultimately a hopeful act. It confirms a bond which already exists, since companionship recognizes and celebrates common, God-given humanity. It is hopeful because it is visionary: a proleptic act which anticipates the future as willed by God. It looks forward beyond the present moment in bringing into being now what could more generally be the case, for more people: better relationship.

Acts of solidarity can only be truly eschatological – signs of God's ultimate acting in and for the world – when they are reflected in actions which disclose a person's refusal to accept the present. Mistreatment of people may sometimes have to be endured. It may have to be experienced by those who show solidarity with the mistreated. But it cannot be accepted as inevitable. Much of human life comprises living with the unsatisfactory nature of things. Not all who need healing, for example, have the necessary access to medical care. Unfairness and injustice exist within the distribution of health care. Solidarity at its fullest includes the challenging of such unfairness and injustice in the face of all signs that it 'may ever be thus'. And however much one might (must) work towards, and support bodies which seek to bring about, better availability of medical care across the world and fairer access to medicines and drugs, there remains the task of being companions of those who wait.[9] Mistreatment exists in many other forms: when people's skills are abused in work, when bodies are scarred by violence, or when minds are tormented by constant criticism. In such contexts, the eschatological presence of Christ is marked by the hopeful act of solidarity. Whenever mistreatment is recognized, but also borne and looked beyond, then Christ's hopeful presence is perceived.

Solidarity takes two forms: companionship with the person who is now mistreated, and solidarity with Jesus whose commitment to his vocation of companionship with the mistreated ended in death. Approaching the narratives about Jesus' death with these insights about solidarity drawn from the earlier parts of the gospel texts prevents the Passion narrative with which each Gospel concludes being seen as about something unique which happened to a man like no other. The immense significance of what happened to Jesus need not be downplayed. It is still right and appropriate to reflect on what God was doing in Jesus, in and through the death, its aftermath and its consequences for Jesus' followers.[10] However, 'living in the light of the stories of Jesus as found in the Gospels' does not just mean trying to be 'Jesus-like'. It is important also to clarify how the whole human story which surrounds the life of Jesus can be 'lived within' by those who follow his way. In the case of responding to the narratives about his death, Jesus' followers have to reckon with the difficulties entailed in acting in solidarity with the mistreated. In this way, the meaning of Jesus' death is not confined to debates about its atoning significance. The symbolic significance of his death, as indicating the extent of human inhumanity and the price of trying to live a truly good life, is also apparent. Living in solidarity with the mistreated acknowledges the scale on which crucifixions continue.

[9] One of the greatest challenges facing the world today is the making available more cheaply throughout the developing world, especially across large parts of Africa, the drugs needed to treat those suffering from HIV/AIDS.

[10] All of which – death, resurrection and discipleship – contributed to the emergence and development of the atonement theories with which Christian tradition has worked and wrestled ever since.

Wherever forgiveness occurs

God in Christ is present wherever forgiveness occurs. 'Forgive us our debts, as we also have forgiven our debtors' (Matt. 6.12) is at the heart of Christian (and most religions') spirituality. In Christian understanding, God is the ground of such forgiveness, being the source of all love. Furthermore, God's forgiveness is bound up with the life, death and resurrection of Jesus Christ. This linking of God's forgiveness with the figure of Jesus Christ indicates that in Christian understanding wherever forgiveness is worked for and received, it is through the God known in Jesus Christ that this occurs, whether those who experience forgiveness are aware of it or not. It is God alone who forgives (Mark 2.7), but forgiveness occurs where Jesus Christ is present (Mark 2.5). As God works in a Christ-like way, it can therefore be assumed that forgiveness always occurs 'in Christ'.

But what does this mean outside of an explicitly Christian, or religious, frame of reference? Does the statement that forgiveness always occurs 'in Christ' really apply to every act of forgiveness? I think it does. The only question we shall need to return to is what, if anything, is added to the experience of forgiveness by its being interpreted as 'in Christ'? In the meantime, the daily forgiving of a child by a parent, or a parent by a child, must be recognized as an example of God's continuing to work in Christ in the world. When an employer says to an employee who has owned up to forgetting to send out a crucial order on time, 'that's OK' and really means it, and the employee can sense that the employer really means it, then either a potential break in a working relationship is prevented, or an actual break is healed. This is forgiveness, enabling restoration of right relationship, in the context of everyday life. It is worthy of much greater respect than it often receives. Indeed, such occurrence of forgiveness may be considered of ultimate significance. For peace and peaceable living will not come about without constant, daily instances of forgiveness happening.

On a broader scale, there are sometimes stories in the news of people who have been badly wronged (for example, physically attacked) publicly forgiving the perpetrators. That such stories are thought newsworthy indicates how unusual and also how difficult such forgiveness is. On a broader scale still, we might think of the many recent examples of public apologies made by politicians on behalf of nations for past actions. As I write, the news tells of the marking of the sixtieth anniversary of the liberation of the Nazi concentration camps. Alongside words of apology are some profound expressions of forgiveness by people who have experienced injustice on an almost unimaginable scale. Holocaust survivors demonstrate that forgiveness does not necessarily entail forgetting. Rather, it is the active refusal to allow a wrongful act wholly to shape the life of the victim, or necessarily to require vengeance upon the perpetrator.[11] Forgiveness is the cutting of what at first seems an inevitable link of cause and effect – and, in Christian understanding, this can only be achieved with God's help.

When people experience a transformation in life

Christians are constantly prone to 'spiritualize': to take the sting out of the very physical aspects of gospel stories which talk of the blind receiving their sight, the lame walking, or hungry people being fed. Sermons that end '. . . and are we not like the blind man?' frequently shift the focus to a metaphorical blindness. Preachers want to remind their congregations of what they are missing that week by not 'seeing' world news in a particular way, or what they are 'blind to' if they remain too comfortable in today's consumerist culture. The permutations are many.

Of course, preachers have to do that, and the Gospels even invite this process. A theme of 'seeing' runs right through the Gospel of John. From the prologue ('we have seen his glory . . .', 1.14), through John the Baptist's witnessing of the baptism of Jesus ('I saw the Spirit . . . I myself have seen . . .', 1.32, 34) and Jesus' invitation to two of John's disciples to 'come and see' (1.39), to Thomas's doubting ('unless I see the mark of the nails in his hands . . .', 20.25) and Jesus' declaration, 'Blessed are those who have not seen and yet have come to believe' (20.29), the Gospel is

---

[11] This is not, of course, to say that appropriate punishment may not be right in criminal cases where harm has been done.

filled with references to sight. And these are not all about physical, literal seeing.

I think we need to be careful not to underestimate the literalness of the Gospels, in a way that suits materially comfortable, healthy contemporary Christians. But we should also be careful not to over-literalize, with the result that we miss the many figurative levels on which the Gospels themselves are inviting us to work.

Many of the gospel stories about Jesus show how meeting him and his movement brought about a transformation in a person's life. For many, the experience of their encounter with Jesus was so overwhelming that they had to tell the world (e.g. Matt. 9.31; Mark 1.45; Luke 13.13). It is understandable that these stories have led much Christian thinking to be focused on 'conversion'. But attention to conversion in its modern sense stifles the stories. Conversion is too cognitive a concept to do them justice ('I did not believe and now I do'). Even if an emotional component is stressed ('I suddenly felt a need to repent', 'I felt a warm glow passing through my body'), this does not always capture what the Gospels describe. Jesus' healings and exorcisms happen in the normal course of life (in homes, on the road), and not at big, staged events, or even (usually) in any identifiable 'religious' settings at all. They do not always occur to those who ask for healing (Matt. 8.5–13; Mark 5.35–43).

The challenge, then, may be as much to examine what it is in human life that genuinely transforms us as to examine the results of any efforts on our part to go and 'look for Jesus' or to 'seek transformation'. Perhaps we should work back from that which transforms us to what we can learn about God in Christ, and what it can mean to participate in Christ. This respects the way that the grace of God appears to work: transformation is always a gift, and always a surprise in the intensity with which it takes effect. Receiving sight when you have not been able to see, walking when you have been lame, cannot but be a life-changing event. And it will impact not just the person transformed, but all those around.

Transformation means 'dramatic change'. It is intriguing that, like the word 'community', it is almost invariably used as a positive term. It sounds like a good thing. Its basic, more neutral, meaning of 'change in form' gets lost in the assumption that the change is always for the better. There is no need to halt this tendency. For when the term is used, say, to indicate that a person has left behind ways of living which were destructive, or has reached a major insight into who they are, or has found a purpose and meaning in life where there seemed to be none before, then this is undoubtedly to be welcomed. The theological task is to facilitate interpretation of such positive change in terms of divine presence and action in Christ.

But people are also transformed in ways that are not always to do with leaving bad things behind: the death of a loved one, an accident, or a debilitating illness. Clearly, such events can be classed more as experiences of suffering or solidarity. Their transforming effect needs noting here nevertheless. At root, calling such experiences instances of transformation reminds us that it is at points of major transition in life that the work of God within the created order may be especially exposed to view. God is discovered as the one who wills the good, and accompanies the struggling and suffering. Yet God knows that the level of freedom granted to creation brings no guarantee that good will always triumph. Those who live in the light of the narratives about Jesus in the Gospels, believing that God is at work for good in the world, do not live with a sense that transformation comes cheap. It is hard work. It is difficult to see. It is even hard to receive as a gift. For it changes lives.

Whenever people discover what they believe to be their true identity

'Authenticity' has proved a fashionable word for anyone influenced by existentialism, be it in a Christian or other form. The notion that a person must truly 'claim' an identity for themselves, by asserting themselves via their particular words and actions, has been profoundly influential.[12] Such an approach coheres directly with any approach to Christian faith which stresses the importance of personal confession of faith. Any act of

---

[12] In Christianity since Kierkegaard, and more generally (in the late twentieth century) through Sartre and Camus.

conscious initiation (believer's baptism, confirmation) links with the notion that authentic human living requires an individual to declare what approach to life they 'own' for themselves. Participation in baptism or confirmation would, however, become an 'inauthentic' act if it were undertaken as 'a matter of course', 'the thing to do', and not truly chosen by the participant.

Stories of people's encounter with Jesus in the Gospels, and especially of the disciples' journeying with Jesus, link the question of whether to follow Jesus and questions of identity (and thus of authenticity) – Jesus' and others'. The Caesarea Philippi story in the Synoptic Gospels (Mark 8.27–30/Matt. 16.13–20/Luke 9.18–20) is crucial in this regard. It is both a powerful narrative in itself, and occupies a pivotal position in the first three Gospels. Here Jesus consults with his disciples about whether his own identity has yet been grasped by the populace and by the disciples themselves. Once Peter identifies Jesus as the Messiah (Mark 8.29), then the disciples are asked whether they are prepared to identify with the kind of Messiah that Jesus is, and whether they are therefore prepared to take their identities from their relationship with him (Mark 8.31—39.1/Matt. 16.21–27/Luke 9.21–27).

It is striking that identity is being derived from identification with and relationship to Jesus. Readers and hearers of the Gospels' texts are invited to consider a form of human living in which they are shaped by an appropriate form of dependence – on God, in Christ, in the context of following. This is authentic living. We may wish to continue to call this 'Christian existentialism'. If so, it cannot mean an approach to human identity or authenticity which would so emphasize human freedom and autonomy that an individual could claim complete independence. Authentic human living will undoubtedly include the free choice as to which groups or traditions we affiliate ourselves. But in the same way as the disciples both chose to follow Jesus when invited, so also any follower chooses to belong, and to be dependent, on the God who calls through Jesus Christ. It can rightly be argued that this is but discovering a relationship with God which God already makes available to us. But authentic living, and the discovery of a true identity, must entail a genuine choosing of relationships in and through which we are who we are. In terms of the discussions of subsequent chapters, it is clear that the way a person inhabits the many social contexts in and through which they live their lives has a direct effect on who and what they experience Christ to be.[13] Christ and (purported) total detachment from any kind of dependence cannot belong together. To be 'in Christ' is to be human, and to be human is to be connected to others. Our identities are bound up with others. In presenting an account of Christian discipleship in the form of the Jesus story, then, the Gospels suggest that there is a direct connection between what it means to be human and what it means to be in Christ.

Whenever truth is told, however painful truth-telling may sometimes prove

Jesus is clearly portrayed in the Gospels as a truth-teller, sometimes uncomfortably, even aggressively so. The accounts of his encounter with the Canaanite/Syro-Phoenician woman (Matt. 15.22–28/Mark 7.24–30), the fig-tree incident (Matt. 21.18–22 parr.) and his having a go at the Scribes and Pharisees (Matt. 23) all make for uneasy reading. In the first case, Jesus wants nothing to do with the woman, but then she tells him a plain truth or two and shakes him out of his exclusivity. So the narrative records how truth-telling happened *between* Jesus and one of his interlocutors. In other words, truth-telling occurs not simply from the mouth of Jesus but in the contexts in which God works, in and through Jesus – even already in the Gospels.

The fig-tree story is one of the most baffling in the Gospels, though surely incorporates an authentic saying of Jesus (for no early Christian would have invented a cursing Jesus). The story is laden with symbolism (e.g. the fig-tree standing for Israel), the detail and ramifications of which cannot be gone into here. Suffice it to say that, given the point at which it appears in Mark's Gospel, the story 'forms a fitting context for Jesus' violent action in the temple'.[14] In other words, it is a prophetic gesture which paves the way for the equally prophetic, but more public, demonstration in the Temple.[15]

[13] Bearing in mind that some of these contexts are *not* chosen (e.g. family).
[14] M. D. Hooker, *The Gospel According to St Mark*, London: A & C Black, 1991, p. 262.
[15] Even more challengingly, Matthew 21.28–32 suggests that actions will always have priority over thoughts and just words.

There is a lengthy collection of harsh words for the Scribes and Pharisees in Matthew 23. Whether or not Matthew gets the Pharisees historically right is not at issue here.[16] Receiving the gospel as it is, readers and hearers have to deal with Jesus as he is presented. This Jesus does not mince his words: 'you lock your people out of the kingdom of heaven . . . you make the new convert twice as much a child of hell as yourselves . . . you are like whitewashed tombs . . . you snakes, you brood of vipers . . .' (Matt. 23.13, 15, 27, 33).

A problem with all such biblical passages, of course, is that they may appear to give licence to anyone who feels they have a prophetic vocation to 'sound off' about what they feel strongly about. Similarly the words of the classical Hebrew prophets invite imitation ('you cows of Bashan . . . who oppress the poor, who crush the needy . . .', Amos 4.1). Prophetic speech is, however, not enough. Nor are isolated words of prophecy. Prophetic speech and action have both to be rooted lest they are presented as detached, isolated rantings of individuals. Prophets are radicals *because* they are rooted.[17] They return to roots and re-work traditions. It is in the examination of their claims to be truthful re-workers of the traditions in which they stand that they are tested in their trustworthiness. The people of God (within which the Christian Church claims its place) is a body out of which prophets constantly emerge (to challenge the Church), which then tests the words of its prophets. Prophets are uncomfortable, and truth-telling is challenging in many directions. But in the clarification of what truth is and where truth is being told, God is certainly at work.

Wherever the abuse of power is challenged

Truth-telling at its best includes challenging the abuse of power. Matthew 23 seethes with the divine mandate to challenge inap-

[16] It is now a commonplace observation that these texts reflect a later (post-70) situation, when disputes may have developed between Christians and Pharisaic Jews. In the time of Jesus, however, though Jesus probably was critical of some Jews, as a Jew himself it may not have been directly critical of Pharisees per se (on this see, e.g., E. P. Sanders, *Jesus and Judaism*, London: SCM Press, 1985, ch. 10). Indeed, it is even possible he was a Pharisee himself.

[17] 'Radical', deriving from the Latin 'radix' (root).

propriate piety and hypocrisy. Jesus embodies this opposition in his practice. The same message is present in Jesus' handling of the squabbles of his own disciples (Mark 9.33–37 and 10.35–45). Jesus is opposing their desire for rank and status. 'If you would simply jettison your concerns about "who's first?"', Jesus is saying, 'then you will have more chance of acting rightly and justly.' Their capacity to challenge the abuse of power is prevented by their own desire to acquire power for themselves.

This insight has the potential of being received in a politically naive way without further scrutiny, as if Jesus had no real grasp of political structures and therefore Christians likewise need not be concerned about organizations and their working. Followers of Jesus clearly have to wrestle with the fact that Jesus sat as loose as he could to formal structures. He may or may not have been a Pharisee (it seems more unlikely than likely) and though he was a loyal Jew (Mark 1.44), it does not appear that he held office of any kind. He called his disciples away from their normal trades, no doubt to their families' utter despair, and so his attacks on the abuse of power are made from a relatively detached social position.

In contemporary life in the West most of us do not have the chance to be like that, or we choose not to be for reasons that are regarded as socially acceptable. We may have families, feel that God wants us to use our skills in the thick of working life, or we may accept the cut and thrust of belonging to a political party. We have to accept, then, that 'challenging the abuse of power' will take forms whose consistency (or not) with the gospel narratives about Jesus may be very hard to recognize. But it is difficult to resist the conclusion that challenging the abuse of power, by various means which remain consistent with the tenor of Jesus' teaching and action, is an aspect of the act of following.

A simple example from the organizational life of a contemporary church can be given here. Much of the work I have been engaged in recently has had to do with clarifying the theological basis on which the Methodist Church structures its own life so that power is properly and appropriately shared and not abused (e.g. between lay and ordained, between presbyters, between presbyters and deacons). The work has included exploration of the overused but rarely defined concept of 'oversight'. An appropriately theological understanding of oversight invites churches to look at how power is wielded and at how individuals who are empowered to exercise authority actually operate within structures of accountability.[18] Without such self-scrutiny churches are more likely to perpetuate practices which abuse power.

To detect the work of God in Christ in the world, and to participate in Christ in this work, we must be committed to challenging the abuse of power. Conversely, wherever the abuse of power is challenged, those seeking to be in Christ will see traces of where God is and what God is doing in and for the world. From such contexts, fresh insights into who Christ is can emerge.

Whenever creativity blossoms

We must not, however, gain the impression that traces of God's work in Christ are mostly to do with times of crisis or with human weakness or sinfulness, with just the odd transforming moment of grace thrown in. The Spirit of God at work throughout the world, identifiable to Christians in the form of Christ, works not only in the power to heal but also in the creation of beauty.

One of the most beautiful stories in the Gospels is about apparent wastefulness. When the woman with the 'alabaster jar of very costly ointment of nard' pours the ointment on Jesus' head (Mark 14.3), there is uproar (14.4–5).[19] Again, symbolic interpretation is

[18] The results of the collaborative work undertaken on this can be found in 'The Nature of Oversight' in *Agenda of the Methodist Conference, Torquay 2005*, Peterborough: Methodist Publishing House, 2005, pp. 60–123 (available in amended form on the Methodist Church's website at www.methodistchurch. org.uk). There has also been much work undertaken recently on how the abuse that happens in society and church is to be understood and countered. See, for example, 'Domestic Abuse' in *Agenda of the Methodist Conference, Torquay 2005*, pp. 398–438, the theological section of which runs from pp. 410 to 428 (also available on the Methodist Church's website). The ecumenical investigation into sexual abuse within churches in Britain and Ireland appeared as *Time for Action: Sexual Abuse, the Churches and a New Dawn for Survivors*, London: CTBI, 2002.

[19] In Luke 7.36–50 the woman is portrayed, by contrast, as anointing Jesus' feet, and the narrative is used differently, i.e., to stress Jesus' willingness to relate to, and forgive, those regarded as socially undesirable. Here in Mark the emphasis is on extravagance. Versions of the story also appear in Matthew 26.6–13, where it is the disciples who kick up the fuss, and John 12.1–8, where the woman is identified as Martha's sister, Mary, and the opponent is Judas Iscariot.

provided ('she has anointed my body beforehand for its burial', 14.8). But we undervalue the significance of this passage if we see only the symbolic meaning: the anticipation of Jesus' death.

The passage is the clearest example in the Gospels that following Jesus may be a frugal affair, but it is not a ruthless, calculating utilitarianism. We need wastefulness in the sense that human beings participate in God in Christ when they find creative ways of disclosing through dramatic, artistic means the joy of living. This joy of living is itself the abundant living to which the Jesus of the Gospel of John refers (John 10.10). Any artistic means through which such joy is celebrated is therefore a potential way in which the presence and activity of God in Christ in the world can be discerned.

Such an insight invites a great debate about how theology or religion and the arts relate, whether all art is God-inspired, whether the arts now challenge religion as a channel through which God is grasped, and so forth. I cannot enter into such discussions here.[20] However, it is worth noting the connection between the apparent wastefulness of artistic endeavour and of time spent in worship. Worship is an extravagance because it has no immediately useful purpose other than enabling those who participate to enter the presence of God. Yes, it can empower. Yes, it can be stimulating. Yes, it can inform and educate. At times it can even entertain, at least in the sense of filling in the odd hour or two in an escapist kind of way.[21] It also functions as a kind of social life. But its main purpose is none of these things. It is, in a very potent sense, a waste of time. It seeks to provide a space for those who participate to be lifted beyond time, in order better to be able to live within it.

[20] For the briefest of introductions to the topic see my article 'Religion and the Arts' in C. Partridge (ed.), *Dictionary of Contemporary Religion in the Western World*, Leicester and Downers Grove: InterVarsity Press, 2002, pp. 65–8. More extensively, see e.g. J. Begbie, *Voicing Creation's Praise: Towards a Theology of the Arts*, Edinburgh: T & T Clark, 1991; F. B. Brown, *Good Taste, Bad Taste and Christian Taste, Aesthetics in Religious Life*, Oxford: Oxford University Press, 2000; and W. Dyrness, *Visual Faith: Art, Theology and Worship in Dialogue*, Baker Academic, 2001.

[21] Again, whether worship is 'entertainment' in any real sense is a question that cannot be entered into here. I have touched briefly on the question in *Cinema and Sentiment: Film's Challenge to Theology*, Milton Keynes: Paternoster Press, 2004, ch. 2.

Worship which is well planned and well prepared draws on similar resources to those used in artistic endeavour. The significant difference is that 'successful' or 'good' worship is never simply the result of exercising artistic skill.[22] But good worship is never prepared without it. Worship includes but is more than the sum of the creativity of those who lead or even of all those who participate in it. Wherever such creative wastefulness exists – be it in the arts or worship – then God in Christ is struggling to find form.

Whenever people renounce reliance on wealth

This next trace of God takes us in a quite different direction. From the woman's wastefulness with nard we move to a theme which runs through the whole gospel tradition, the Synoptic Gospels especially: hostility to wealth.[23] Jesus is portrayed as particularly hostile to those who put their trust in wealth. Jesus' conversation with the rich man who could not bring himself to part with his possessions (Mark 10.17–22/Matt. 19.16–30/Luke 18.18–30) and the story of the rich fool who kept on building bigger barns to store his wealth (Luke 12.13–21) are just two examples of Jesus' truth-telling that focus on how people rely on material wealth, at cost to their attention to what matters more (the inheritance of eternal life – Mark 10.17). One's life 'does not consist in the abundance of possessions' (Luke 12.15) could even be regarded as a summary version of Jesus' gospel.

I mentioned earlier that following Jesus may well be a frugal affair. Jesus certainly commended such an approach to life, especially for his immediate disciples. When they travelled they were to take very little with them see, (for example, Matt. 10.9–10).[24]

---

[22] Arguably 'good' art is never simply this either. But this issue, too, must be for another time.

[23] For a comprehensive treatment of this topic, see T. E. Schmidt, *Hostility to Wealth in the Synoptic Gospels*, Sheffield: Sheffield Academic Press, 1987.

[24] This and other passages form the basis of the contemporary discussion about the social standing of the Jesus movement, and whether or not he and his followers had any link with Cynic philosophers who operated similarly frugally. On this, see, for example, G. Theissen, *Social Reality and the Early Christians: Theology, Ethics and the World of the New Testament*, Edinburgh: T & T Clark, 1992, chs. 1–2; F. G. Downing, *Cynics and Christian Origins*, Edinburgh: T & T Clark, 1992; J. D. Crossan, *Jesus: A Revolutionary Biography*, San Francisco: HarperSanFrancisco, 1994, ch. 5.

The notorious interpretation of the parable of the Good Samaritan offered by Margaret Thatcher (he could not have helped the injured man by paying the inn-keeper had he not generated enough wealth to do so) is at some distance from this level of material detachment.[25]

Asceticism is not going to be the call of many. But the challenge of the gospel narratives may be less that of the tough test of whether we can all be followers in the mould of the apostolic mission, than whether we can do justice to the Gospels' more general attack on wealth-reliance.

Everyone needs something to live on. And even the anointing woman had spare nard. So there is room even in the Gospels for some frivolity and extravagance. The woman's nard does not justify opulence, well-above average salaries, a refusal to spend on any but one's nearest and dearest, or ownership of multiple (mostly empty) properties. The 'hostility to wealth' strand of the gospel tradition continues to challenge us about how we use the wealth that we have. The moment that we betray, by our words or actions, that our wealth accumulation or our patterns of consumption matter more to us than anything, then we begin to put ourselves out of Christ's sphere of influence. We are choosing not to let the words of the Gospels reach us. The moment that we begin to question what we are doing with our wealth and why, and choose to act in a way that may benefit others, then our hesitation or refusal to rely on material wealth become a sign that God in Christ is challenging us. Such a challenge is wholly in continuity with the gospel narratives.

At meal-times

The final trace of the presence and activity of God in Christ that I am looking at may seem tame by comparison with the others. I am, however, convinced that this motif is crucial both in the gospel tradition and for the task of refreshing and rediscovering viable forms of social living in the present.

Much of Jesus' activity, as portrayed in the Gospels, occurred in

---

[25] 'No one would have remembered the Good Samaritan if he'd only had good intentions. He had money as well' (from a 1980 television interview, cited on the BBC TV website http://news.bbc.co.uk/1/hi/uk_politics/1888444.stm).

the context of meals. Jesus was known to like his food and drink (Matt. 9.14–15; 11.19; John 2.1–11), he frequented people's homes (Matt. 8.14) and ate with whoever was there (Matt. 9.10). In Luke's account of 'the mission of the seventy', eating habits even appear to be part of the missionary strategy: 'Remain in the same house, eating and drinking whatever they provide' (Luke 10.7).[26] There were concerns whenever Jesus and his disciples could not eat (Mark 3.20; 6.31), and Jesus was certainly hungry at times (Mark 11.12). He turned one significant meal-time into one that the Christian Church would then make its central, symbolic meal – the Eucharist (Matt. 26.26–30, parr.). Eating habits therefore were – and are – crucial for understanding how and where God in Christ is present in the world.

Two obvious points should be stressed. First, eating is often a social activity. Jesus was able to turn this everyday practice into a context for celebrating the presence of God's reign simply by virtue of breaking taboos about who you could or should eat with. By eating with prostitutes and tax-collectors, and encouraging his followers to do likewise, he modelled new forms of social interaction.

Second, appreciation of food is an expression of gratitude for the givenness of the earth. When Jesus blessed the loaves and the fish donated by the boy before the crowd of thousands (Mark 6.41), he was doing no more than 'saying grace'. But the act, then as now, signifies that sharing in a meal can always be more than the functional refreshment of our bodies. It is an occasion for thanksgiving and a site of potentially profound interaction between those who share in the meal.

The Gospels are thus again suggesting where a trace of God's action in the world may be found today. This final trace is, however, perhaps especially difficult to recognize. In the age of fish fingers and the TV dinner, and a 'meal-time' as a sequential event as different members of a household take up their position on the sofa at different times of the evening, it is difficult to gain any sense of a meal as a social occasion for thanksgiving and interaction. Interestingly, there has been much discussion recently about

[26] J. D.Crossan, *The Historical Jesus: The Life of a Mediterranean Jewish Peasant*, San Francisco: HarperSan Francisco, 1991, pp. 341–4.

the social loss of 'Sunday lunch' in British society. It would surely not be appropriate to try to summon up nostalgically the 'roast meat and two veg' family idyll of the 1950s. But it is being recognized that much is lost when households do not share food together on a regular basis. Family meals, for example, are often flashpoints, sites of conflict in a family's life. But they are all the more important for that, as they enable family members to confront (and, if possible, talk through) what would otherwise be avoided. Likewise, the meals recorded in the Gospels became flashpoints, not only for those involved, but as symbols of the patterns of social inclusion and exclusion in first-century Palestinian society.

The fragmented body of Christ: responding to the ethical challenge of doing Christology

This chapter has looked at a number of key examples of where the shape of Christ is discernible in contemporary life. Reflection on the Gospels enabled identification of that shape of Christ. Four important observations will now need to be borne in mind in the chapters that follow.

Beyond individualism

First, what has been supplied in this chapter are 'types' or 'occasions' of God's presence and activity in Christ, as evidenced in everyday settings. But it is not yet clear how such action is possible in institutional contexts. It still looks as though these actions are the work of individuals. The significance of undertaking such actions in different contexts (e.g. in the worlds of employment, education, family, church or political life) has not yet been explored. The manner of God's presence in the world in Christ may have been identified with reference to a range of narratives about Jesus. But the impression could have been left that it is up to individuals alone to make such links, and offer such interpretations of contemporary life. Doesn't such an approach fragment the body of Christ in the world and mean that identification of the presence of Christ is subject to the interpretative skills of individuals? It may be a basic error to confine an understanding of Christ's body in the world only to the church. But to define the presence and activity of God in Christ in the world by means of a collection of isolated moments would also be mistaken. It would fail to acknowledge how human life is lived.

Christ and church

Second, therefore, what is the role in all this of the social institution 'church'? It is clear from the examples given that God is present in Christ in the world not merely in the form of 'church'. But as a counter to individualism, it will be necessary to clarify the role played by the church as a social form of Christ. It will also be necessary to show how the church interrelates with other social forms in which Christ may be deemed present in the world. For very little has been said thus far in this study either about other social forms in which the 'shape' or 'traces' of Christ have been discerned, or about the social, political and economic contexts within which such a discernment process takes place.[27] Addressing the concerns identified in these first two remarks about individualism and church, then, is a means of carrying through a Christocentric approach to practical theology. It is also a way of doing this without succumbing to the distortions of egoism and ecclesiocentrism.[28]

Life, not Christian life

Third, it is clear that the danger of Christian imperialism will always be present when practical Christian theology is undertaken. We are dealing with life here, not church life, or the Christian life. It is true that the moment life events are reflected upon, and given shape in some narrative form, a particular inter-

[27] Indeed, I think there has been too little said in the history of Christian theology about the social form of Christ beyond the church. This makes the practical challenge issued by Bonhoeffer's work all the more important.

[28] On these two distortions of Christocentrism, see *Christ in Focus*, ch. 3. Egoism is there defined in relation to undue emphasis upon the *pro me* aspect of soteriology. Here, the emphasis shifts to the individual Christian observer potentially being the only beneficiary of such theological reflection. But the end result is the same: Christology is not being done for the sake of others as well as self.

pretative world comes into play.[29] Hence my use of the term 'in Christian understanding' at many points in this chapter. Use of the term also indicates the particular, and limited, task that I am engaged in. This is a *Christian* theological exercise. It is offered as a reading of human experience on the basis of a Christian reading of the world. It *is* presented as a reading of experience not only confined to Christians. In this sense it is offered to a wider public, and not just for the use of already Christian people. Such an approach acknowledges that forgiveness, solidarity with the mis-treated, transformation, sharing meals, and so on, occur outside Christianity, including within other religious traditions. It accepts that other accounts (religious and not) will be given as to 'what is actually going on' in the examples of life experience described above. And so the offering of a Christian theological account of such life experience is made not to claim the event or to suggest that a Christian account is inevitably and immediately more truthful than any other.[30] Rather, the intent is to invite reflection on what is happening in life. Christological interpretation of life experience, which occurs through the juxtaposition of gospel nar-ratives and contemporary events, simply channels such reflection along important tracks (forgiveness, solidarity, human flourish-ing, handling suffering, etc.). Without such interpretation – which Christianity can offer to public discourse – these important aspects of human life may be damagingly ignored.

---

[29] Indeed, it can be argued that an interpretative world has already shaped the thought processes used when a person reflects on a life experience. I cannot develop this discussion fully here. I must simply record my view that though all experiences are indeed 'traditioned', the fact that some experiences cause us to review (and sometimes change substantially) our world views, and on occasions very surprisingly and suddenly, at least means that our cognitive worlds do not wholly control us. Even if changes in world view may be traceable to clashing cognitive worlds, and there really is no such thing as 'raw experience', it remains true also that not all reality is cognitive.

[30] Much is indeed being claimed for a Christian interpretation. But its own truth may need to be augmented by the accounts of others, which can in turn be informed and fed by a Christian reading. This, it seems to me, is the essence of inter-disciplinary work which occurs under the banner of 'practical' or 'pastoral' theology, theological reflection informed by biblical, systematic and philosophi-cal insight, but also from other disciplines such as psychology, sociology and anthropology, as well as religious studies.

The purpose of theology

The question inevitably arises: what is added to the life experiences identified? Does a Christian interpretation, and the accompanying invitation to others to engage in theological discussion, enrich the accounts offered from other sources about what happens in daily living? To express this question much more bluntly: what on earth is theology for?

For theology to have any real purpose in society, it must show how the traditions it carries and the methods it uses might be of benefit both to people within the Christian tradition and to those beyond it. This is not mere utilitarianism. If Christians are not to see themselves as living within a self-contained, and tightly sealed, world, then it must be possible for them to explain the value of their interpretation of life to others. And it should be possible for this to be done in a way which demonstrates how Christian interpretation contributes to a fuller understanding of human life.

As we turn to explore what concrete social forms Christ takes in the world today, in the light of the above observations, we shall need to:

- appreciate the public role of Christian theology;
- resist all tendencies of any group, churches included, to suggest that who Christ is and what God in Christ is doing are fully grasped from the outset;
- respect the way in which God speaks and acts in the world today through the many social forms in which Christ is present.

We shall be doing all these three things in the following chapters.

3   Race, nation and ethnicity: Christ in whatever state we're in

Christ and the human race

Human beings live in groups and within many social networks, large and small. However tenuous these social links may seem or be, they are decisive for who we are as people. The widespread concern prevalent in the West in the present time about social fragmentation derives from the loss of respect for these groups and networks. Examining Christ in relation to diverse forms of social life in order to clarify Christ's social forms, and Christ's contribution to the shaping of truly human life, is thus part of the opposition to contemporary social fragmentation.

The first form to be considered is the human race. It is likely that the terms 'race' and 'racism' will go on being used when what is in fact at issue is the nature and quality of relationship between people of different ethnicity, culture or colour. However, it would be preferable for theological reasons to reserve the term 'race' for the whole of humanity. There is, on this understanding, only one race: the human race, created by God. On this basis it is possible to declare that all human beings are equal.

There are two problems with an approach to humanity's unity that wishes to speak of only one race. First, such an approach can in practice become a means of playing down ethnic diversity. In expressing an intent to treat all equally, we may at the same time take our own particular context and origin so much as the norm that we neglect to pay any real attention to difference. For instance, when a white speaker in a British context wishes to use the term 'race' to refer to the whole of humankind, it may simply mean, in practice, that he or she is overlooking the cultures and backgrounds of people from Asian, African-Caribbean, Chinese or other ethnic origins. Religious difference, as one form of ethnic diversity, may also be given little room. A second problem, therefore, is that considering Christ as taking form in the one human race can become yet another thinly veiled form of Christian imperialism.

Though such dangers exist, there are two main, positive reasons for pursuing the idea of Christ taking form across the whole human race. On the one hand, it reminds Christian theologians that they are dealing with beliefs and ideas that are not solely of concern to the Christian community. Christian theology arises from and is composed in the service of Christian communities around the world. But in the truth-claims it makes, it offers an interpretation of human experience that extends beyond that of Christians alone. Christian theology cannot expect immediate support for its ideas and insights from anyone outside of Christian communities. But it is seeking interest and respect from any who will listen and seek to learn as it offers its readings of reality.

On the other hand, seeking to interpret Christ in relation to the human race as a whole challenges Christian theologians to reinterpret one of Christianity's key concepts: the body of Christ. In Christian theology the church is identified as Christ's body. This produces problems on two fronts. How can the church as we know it be prevented from getting above itself? How can Christianity be prevented from seeking to absorb the whole of creation into itself (as the church) in its desire to see the created order become as God wants it to be? The latter danger, of course, is merely exacerbated when Christ is interpreted in relation to humanity as a whole. But rather than run away from the difficulty, Christian theology would do well to accept the challenge to redefine the body of Christ in a pluralist age.

The nature of the challenge is this. Participation in Christ entails being involved in something fundamental about what it means to be human. But how is the sense that a universal aspect of humanity is being grasped christologically to be maintained without suggesting that any particular parochial form of Christianity has discovered and said all that can be said about Christ? In fact, if Christ exists in multiple social forms in the

world, then new things are always being discovered from participation in the many forms in and through which Christ is encountered.

All that said, there remains a basic difficulty with noting the
link between Christ and the human race: no one except God has
an overview of humanity. The notion of humanity's unity cannot
but be God's perspective, and the goal of God's creation. It is
clearly not a present reality. In current experience, human beings
participate in a fractured humanity. To call the church 'the body
of Christ' is to participate consciously in a social form of living
which acknowledges this brokenness, while also celebrating in
anticipation the fact that God saves and will go on renewing the
creation. But may this not be true of other social forms of Christ's
existence? The church is then illustrative of other efforts to anticipate the restoration of humanity. To put this another way: the
healing of the fractured body of Christ, as reflected in a disunited
human race, is difficult to grasp unless humanity itself is considered in terms of more manageable and tangible sub-forms. The
restoration of the body of Christ is an eschatological vision. God's
vision for humanity and the healing of the broken body of Christ
can converge. But this can only come in God's time. Human participation in this occurs via small steps, and in humble ways.

As a concept, then, the 'human race' cannot serve as a practical
theological category in the same way as many of the other social
forms of human living which will now be examined. Its value is
as an overarching concept within which all the complex forms of
social life in which Christ may take shape are to be understood.

Christ and the state

At first glance, examining the concept of Christ taking shape as
the 'nation' or the 'state'[1] may seem an unpromising line of

---

[1] There is admittedly an important discussion which could be engaged in here
about the distinction between the terms 'nation', 'state' and the composite
'nation state'. This would be essential in the development of a fuller political
theology. Such nuancing is , however, not necessary to my argument. By referring to 'nation' or 'state' I am acknowledging that in practice such terms are in
common English usually used interchangeably. In Britain people rightly refer
to 'the four nations' (England, Northern Ireland, Scotland and Wales), though
when people say 'in our nation', it is admittedly usually only the English who

enquiry. For surely no one would now claim any close relationship between the social form of Christ and a national political structure. 'Christendom' may have existed after the Edict of Milan of 313, and a relationship between Christ and an imperial structure may have resulted. But this has surely long gone, along with its lingering traces, despite the continued existence of alliances of different forms between church and state in some Northern European countries. The more widespread development of secular democracies is now the norm, not only in the developed world. And where any formal alliances between Christianity and the state do exist, they are links between one religion's institution or institutions (church/churches) and the state. Only in very attenuated form (and from the religious side of the alliance) might this seriously be considered as a relationship between Christ and the state. And yet some aspects of the relationship between Christ and the state do merit scrutiny even now.

Bonhoeffer on church and state

Dietrich Bonhoeffer had a high view both of the state and of the church's role in relation to it. It was because of this that his life as a martyr unfolded in the way it did. The function of Christology in Bonhoeffer's thought is crucial. As we saw in the first chapter, Bonhoeffer's practical theology is utterly Christocentric. On the one hand, Bonhoeffer speaks of 'Christ existing as community.'[2] On the other hand, he reminds readers of his *Ethics* that all created things

> are through and for Christ and exist only in Christ (Col. 1.16). This means that there is nothing, neither persons nor things, which stands outside the relation to Christ. Indeed, it is only in relation to Christ that created things have their being. This

---

are referring both to the nation and the state (England *and* the UK). Scottish and Welsh citizens may distinguish nation from state quite sharply. But I need simply note, as a parochial Englishman, that I am referring here to the relationship between Christ as reality and concept and the basic national political structure within which any reader lives.

[2] Chapter 1, n. 13.

is true not only of man [*sic*] but also of the state, economy, science, nature, etc.[3]

Admittedly, he also explains:

there is no question here of a 'Christian state' or a 'Christian economy', but only of the rightful state and the rightful economy as a secular institution for the sake of Christ.[4]

What Bonhoeffer is doing here is bringing Christ into the closest possible alignment with the state, while asserting that no state can claim identity with Christ, for ultimately the state is subject to Christ's rule. The state's crucial role in enabling Christ to take shape in the world ('as community') is acknowledged. It is for this reason that the corruption of the state's purpose brought about in Germany under National Socialism was so abhorrent to Bonhoeffer. But no state, however supportive it might be of the church, can in itself be a form of Christ.

Bonhoeffer does make an important linguistic distinction in his *Ethics* when he identifies the four 'mandates' that need to be explored.[5] Although he explores the role of the state in Part III of his *Ethics*, he names the four mandates (tasks required by God) as 'labour, marriage, government and the Church'.[6] The 'state' and 'government' are thus distinguished by Bonhoeffer. As Ruth Zerner notes, it is the government, rather than the state, which for Bonhoeffer carries a theological responsibility – that is, which has a divine mandate. As Bonhoeffer says, 'Government is divinely ordained authority to exercise worldly dominion by divine right. Government is deputyship for God on earth.'[7] 'Government' thus carries theological weight as a concept. But the theological responsibility of government also means that it is to be subject to

---

[3] D. Bonhoeffer, *Ethics*, London: SCM Press, 1955, p. 288.

[4] Bonhoeffer, *Ethics*, p. 288.

[5] On the concept of 'mandates' in Bonhoeffer's thought, see above ch. 1, p. 15.

[6] Bonhoeffer, *Ethics*, p. 73.

[7] Bonhoeffer, *Ethics*, p. 297. Zerner notes a distinction between Bonhoeffer's use of the concept of government and his 'previous reliance on "state"' ('Church, State and the "Jewish Question"' in J. De Gruchy (ed.), *The Cambridge Companion to Dietrich Bonhoeffer*, Cambridge: Cambridge University Press, pp. 190–205, here p. 199). There is something in this, though: despite the seemingly clear distinction between 'state' and 'government' in Section III of the *Ethics*, Bonhoeffer's use of the terminology at other points remains ambiguous.

the closest scrutiny, and liable to challenge through active opposition (whether by groups or individuals) to a government's
ideals and actions. Through a government's openness to such
scrutiny and opposition, as Zerner notes, room is left 'for an individual to reject a particular government, while being loyal to the
nation-state'.[8] Meanwhile, there may remain in Bonhoeffer's
thought an 'almost mystical link between church and state'.[9]

Bonhoeffer's approach will prove instructive in due course. He
recognizes that Christian theology cannot overlook the crucial
role played by the state (and/or government) in all human life.
The other mandates he goes on to explore (labour, marriage,
church[10]) cannot but be directly affected by macro-political decisions. But areas of puzzlement remain in his procedure. I shall
mention just two.

First, the distinction between state and government is helpful
with respect to the basic point made (one can still support a
nation or state while opposing a particular government).
However, why permit the concept of nation or state to become
somehow supra-historical (Zerner's identification of the 'mystical
link'), as if beyond time, and outside of human politics? There is
a surprising element of idealism in Bonhoeffer's thinking at this
point, which runs counter to his intent to 'live completely in the
world'.[11] If, then, Zerner is right, the mysticism is of a surprisingly
non-worldly kind. As such, I suggest, it contributes to
Bonhoeffer's failure to develop as fully as he might have how
church, state and government contribute to the shaping of the
forms of Christ that are evident in the mandates of labour, family,
church, marriage, friendship and culture.[12]

Second, it is worth noting, alongside his 'high views' of
state/government and of church, the distinction that Bonhoeffer
sees between the two institutions. Each has its own clear sphere

---

[8] Zerner, 'Church, State', p. 199.

[9] Zerner, 'Church, State', p. 194, referring to Bonhoeffer's writings of 1933.

[10] And other realms of life which sometimes also appear in Bonhoeffer's lists of
mandates: family, culture (i.e., art, friendship and play).

[11] '[I]t is only be by living completely in the world that one learns to have faith' (D.
Bonhoeffer, *Letters and Papers from Prison*, London: SCM Press, 1971, p. 369).

[12] Here one must acknowledge directly that, had he lived beyond 1945, these are
precisely the kinds of loose ends that Bonhoeffer would have been able to pick
up, and work with further.

of operation. This may be regarded as 'typically Lutheran', reflecting the Lutheran doctrine of the two kingdoms (this world and the next).[13] If, however, the state itself is mystically united with the church in Bonhoeffer's thought, then it is not clear whether it is church or state which anticipates the future Kingdom. More fully, as Zerner rightly notes, Bonhoeffer is reliant on a combination of 'themes from the sixteenth-century Reformation, the tradition of German organic political theories of the nineteenth century, and the striving for community and wholeness so evident in his generation (of the Weimar era)'.[14] Whatever its origins, however, Bonhoeffer allows a clear and complicating ambiguity to persist in his thought here. For, by using the state/government distinction as he has, and yet allowing a mystical understanding of the state to hover supra-temporally over his endeavours, he compromises his efforts. His attempt to work out in the most radically contextual and concrete forms possible what it means to be 'church' or be 'in Christ' is stifled to some extent. Only by accepting the full historicity of both concepts (state and church) would Bonhoeffer have been able to develop christological interpretations of all of the 'mandates' he identifies.[15]

These objections notwithstanding, it is still valuable to discuss Bonhoeffer's grappling with these issues. That 'Christ' and 'state' can still be brought alongside each other *at all* in a post-Christendom age is telling.[16] It is imperative to respect all

---

[13] On Luther's doctrine of the two kingdoms, see, for example, Bernhard Lohse, *Martin Luther's Theology: Its Historical and Systematic Development*, Edinburgh: T & T Clark, 1999, chs. 16 and 33. For a contemporary appropriation and critique of the doctrine, see, for example, D. Thompson, *Crossing the Divide: Luther, Feminism and the Cross*, Minneapolis: Augsburg Fortress, 2004, ch. 2.

[14] Zerner, 'Church, State', p. 198.

[15] One could add at this point that this must apply to the theological concept of the Kingdom of God also. The Kingdom/reign of God remains a theological concept and a vision of the future (never to be seen as fully realized or realizable in any human institution, not even as the church). It must nevertheless be recognized as taking some historical form (however inadequate and incomplete) lest it become an abstract, unreal and ultimately unusable concept.

[16] Bonhoeffer deserves great credit for anticipating some of the concerns now pre-occupying theologians (see e.g. the sentences immediately prior to his famous 'who is Christ for us today?' quote, where he writes: 'You would be surprised, and perhaps even worried, by my theological thoughts and the conclusions that they lead to . . .'). His perception of the looming crisis of belief, and the resulting

dimensions of life, including the explicitly political, which impinge upon the concrete, institutional forms that Christ is deemed to take. This applies whether our context is a state in which church and state remain in close alliance (e.g. the UK), or one in which religious convictions and state affairs are kept apart (e.g. the USA).

Working insights

What, then, are the practical consequences of this discussion of Bonhoeffer for the present enquiry? First, in the modern (or post-modern) world, there can be no such thing as a Christian state. Religious plurality is here to stay and this must be reflected in the ways that states do their business. Church and state might work in the closest alliance, but because the two can never be equated, and because religions other than Christianity have an equal claim to work in such alliance, a Western state today can only realistically be religiously plural.

But, second, there can be no wholly secular state either. Though it is easy to refer to 'secular democracy' as the form of government to which many states aspire, all states need to know and make clear how they are going to handle the activity of the religions to which at least some of their citizens are committed. Societies have no need to try to rid themselves of religion, because it is simply not possible. Religions may spring up and die, or may mutate, but it is clear that they do not go away. Even if they are suppressed or wane in popularity, they still persist, or religiosity is diverted into substitute forms. Western secularity has proved to be but skin-deep.

Third, it would be unwise to make any claim that a state could embody Christ. I shall continue to make much, as I did throughout *Christ in Focus*, of a clear distinction between Christ and Christianity, and between Christ and the church. It seems to me

---

radicalism of his thinking, are plain, even if the adoption of his work by 'death of God' theologians in the 1960s is now recognized to have been something of an aberration. On 'post-Christendom' as a current context for being church and doing theology, see, for example, M. Atkins, *Preaching in a Cultural Context*, Peterborough: Foundery Press, 2001. I have explored our current context for doing theology in the West in *Christianity in a Post-Atheist Age*, London: SCM Press, 2002.

quite clear that the activity and presence of God in Christ cut across, and move beyond, both Christianity as a religion, and its social, institutional form as a collection of churches.[17] It would therefore be possible to say that a religiously plural state, in its ideals, beliefs, policies and actions, was reflecting the embodiment of God in Christ in a range of institutional forms. The moment that the notion of 'body of Christ' is not linked to 'church' alone, then multiple social forms in which God in Christ is present in human affairs need to be identified. Furthermore, the healing of the fractured body of Christ is then sought, not only in direct relation to the concept of church, but with respect to a broader range of examples of social and political practice.

The work of the state must certainly be broken down into other forms (e.g. into the way people are supported in their structuring of families and households). But it undoubtedly deserves closer christological scrutiny (how are a government's policies recognizing and fostering the quality of human relationships which reflect what it means to be 'in Christ'?). Significant and subtle shifts of thought would be necessary to prevent the notion of Christ's embodiment in the state becoming the 'Christianization' of the state. Concentrating on this would waste emotional and intellectual energy which could be used elsewhere: in helping to foster the (smaller, more local) social forms in which the embodiment of Christ is better celebrated. Though it is right to examine the way in which Christology affects human societies, the danger of Walter Rauschenbusch's strategy (encapsulated in the title of his 1912 book *Christianizing the Social Order*) should not go unheeded.[18]

This discussion of what the state's existence and activity entail for the social forms in which Christ is embodied in society today therefore points us in new directions. It is to other 'mandates', indeed also some of Bonhoeffer's 'spheres of freedom', that we shall need to turn our attention.[19] Family, marriage, labour, culture (and friendships too) become focal points for scrutiny of the social forms of Christ today. Zerner asks in her discussion of

[17] This insight lay behind the enquiry into the many forms of distortion of Christocentrism in Christian theology identified in Chapter 3 of *Christ in Focus*.
[18] On this, see *Christ in Focus*, ch. 5, esp. p. 137.
[19] On 'spheres of freedom', see above, ch. 1, p. 15.

Bonhoeffer: 'For Bonhoeffer, family and friendship remained as sustaining "mandates". But is that adequate?'[20] This is a question to which we shall need to return.

Christ and ethnicity

Before looking at these other mandates more closely, in Chapters 4 and 5, I need to address one further overarching concept. What role and significance does ethnicity have in relation to the task of clarifying where the presence and activity of God in Christ may be discerned today? Basically, how does a person's ethnic origin affect both their understanding of Christ and the way in which they participate in the social form of Christ?

In *Christ in Focus* I identified ethnocentrism as one of the distortions of Christocentrism in theology. I noted that it is not possible to have a culture-less Christ. Inevitably, all believers operate with some sense that Christ belongs to the people out of which they come. Ethnicity is crucial to human identity – and is therefore, likewise, an essential aspect of Christian identity. Ethnicity only develops into a problematic ethnocentrism in Christology 'when a particular people has so identified itself with Christ that its own activities and beliefs become normative in Christology and the many ways in which Christ needs to be understood and expressed become stifled'.[21]

In this present section of my enquiry, however, the positive aspect of ethnicity in Christology requires greater attention. At root, considering ethnicity in Christology means looking at how Christology handles the relationship between universality and particularity. On the one hand, especially when Jesus is portrayed in visual form, a choice has to be made about how to portray Jesus' ethnicity.[22] Jesus the Christ is thus presented as Chinese, Asian, Black, Maori, White or whatever. Chinese, Asian, Black, Maori or White European Christians are thereby affirmed in their

---

[20] Zerner, 'Christ, State', p. 200.

[21] *Christ in Focus*, p. 64.

[22] This could, of course, be deemed one of the drawbacks of Christianity's commitment to incarnation (!), or at least its refusal to forbid visual images of the figure in whom it sees God. On the other hand, such visual Christologies bring out into the open aspects that word Christologies usually hide.

own ethnic identity by the Christ portrayed. It need not be assumed that this self-relating feature of Christology is inevitably intended to relate directly to the historicity of Jesus of Nazareth. In other words, to use some of the examples cited, no claim is necessarily being made that Jesus *was* Chinese or Maori. These are, after all, faith images. The need for Jesus to be portrayed in ethnically specific terms does, however, serve as a reminder of Jesus' own particularity: he did have a specific context and ethnic background (as a Palestinian Jew).

On the other hand, it is Jesus the universal Christ who is being portrayed, and so, from the perspective of Christian faith, such portrayals also rise above their ethnic specificity. Though portrayed in a particular ethnic form, Jesus is still able to save all people. Likewise, though affirmed in their ethnic identity by visual images of a Jesus 'like them', Christians are reminded by other images that Jesus saves people who are unlike them. In this way they experience the force of Paul's insight in Galatians 3.28 ('There is no longer Jew or Greek, there is no longer slave or free, there is no longer male and female, for all of you are one in Christ Jesus'). Ethnic origin is far from denied. It remains vital to who people are. But participation in Christ brings people into new bonds of relationship, which are no longer defined in terms of ethnicity alone.[23]

This insight is a challenge to national and ethnically based churches. It is a proven finding in church growth theory (the Homogeneous Unit Principle) that people attract others who are similar to them. It is also an inevitable feature of immigration that groups either congregate in the same parts of cities or, if that is not possible, create town- or city-wide associations which enable them to meet (for example, the African-Caribbean Community Group, the Polish Society). Churches are no exception to this rule (the Chinese Church, the Punjabi-Speaking Congregation). On a larger scale, one need only think of the development of Christianity across North America (Lutherans in Minnesota, Baptists in the South, Black Pentecostal Churches in Harlem, Methodism in Georgia and the Carolinas) to be aware of how far-reaching are the effects of such patterns.

---

[23] We must leave aside at this point the possible charge against Paul that he seems strangely unmoved by the fact that being a slave or free is rather different from being either Jew or Greek, or male or female.

At present in Britain, mainstream denominations owning church buildings that can be hired out to other Christian groups are faced with the decision whether to support all lettings to new Christian congregations, especially those that are ethnically based. From one perspective the answer appears simple: lettings should be actively supported for so many obvious reasons. This is an act of hospitality (and these groups pay rent, after all!) Solidarity is being expressed with a group of immigrant Christians trying to find its feet in a new place. Both Christian faith and ethnic identity are thereby being affirmed. Furthermore, this may also be an important ecumenical encounter if the congregation concerned is of a different Christian tradition.

On the other hand, might this be to overlook the difficulty and challenge of really walking together in Christ with people who are different? At the point where it seems wholly right to affirm difference and particularity, the universality of Christ presents a powerful challenge to contemporary believers' participation in Christ in a concrete, social form, when the 'social form' may so emphasize ethnicity that ethnic background becomes a cause of divisiveness. Christ's challenge to exclusiveness invites people both to value difference and to seek what makes for common humanity. Here is the challenge of what it means to be 'church'. A church that recognizes what it truly means to be a form of the body of Christ cannot simply be a collection of ethnically monochrome social groups.[24]

The important relationship between particularity and universality in Christology can be sharpened by an example once more from Bonhoeffer. Writing on his first visit to the USA (in 1930), he remarked: 'If it has come about that today the "black Christ" has to be led into the field against the "white Christ" by a young negro poet, then a deep cleft in the church of Jesus Christ is indicated.'[25] His concern is with Christ's universality, and with

---

[24] Not every church community can be multi-racial, all-age and bring together people of difference social and educational backgrounds, of course. The point here is that it is too easy (a 'cop out' indeed) to say that the church is diverse 'as a whole', without accepting the challenge of working out what it means to be a corporate body of real people who may differ radically from each other. There is a cost involved in actually facing the implications of real difference.

[25] D. Bonhoeffer, *No Rusty Swords*, London: Collins, 1965, p. 112. In the background lay an essay Bonhoeffer wrote on Johnson's *Autobiography of an Ex-Colored Man* (E. Bethge, *Dietrich Bonhoeffer: A Biography* (rev. edn), Minneapolis: Fortress Press, 2000, p. 150).

the absolutizing of a particular interpretation of Christ, a danger all too apparent to him in his own German context. Bonhoeffer's point can be heard as meaning that the 'Black Christ' is an illegitimate development in Christian thought. In context, it is clear that Bonhoeffer is using his experience of being confronted with the Black Christ as a stark reminder of the contextual specificity of all theology. He can also see, however, that while particularity and incarnation go together God is concretely present, contextual particularity can equally lead to the idolization of one's own context or one's own people. He is shaken to recognize the dangerous effects of the particular versions of the 'White Christ' in 1930s Germany.

More than three decades later, in a different setting yet with the same concern for Christ's universality, James Cone can be found arguing that the Black Christ needs to be respected, so that Black Christians see how their own oppression participates in the suffering of Christ. His words offer a critique of Bonhoeffer's perhaps understandable caution:

> maybe our white theologians are right when they insist that I have overlooked the *universal* significance of Jesus' message. But I contend that there is no universalism that is not particular. Indeed their insistence upon the universal note of the gospel arises out of their own particular political and social interests. As long as they can be sure that the gospel is *for everybody*, ignoring that God liberated a *particular* people from Egypt, came in a particular man called Jesus, and for the particular purpose of liberating the oppressed, then they can continue to talk in theological abstractions, failing to recognize that such talk is not the gospel unless it is related to the concrete freedom of the little ones.[26]

Bonhoeffer and Cone set the parameters of the debate as to how 'big pictures' of human being and society in turn affect the understanding and portrayal of Christ. We are shaped by ethnicity (as we are by being human, and by our national identities). But ethnicity does not of itself lead us to understand who Christ is,

---

[26] J. Cone, *God of the Oppressed*, New York: Seabury Press, 1975, p. 137.

and thus who we are. Nor does it define at best what it means to be 'in Christ'. Once again, for the third time in this chapter, we are drawn to the necessity to consider other mandates in our search for forms of Christ in the world.

Summary

This chapter has focused on three large concepts which invite examination when the question of the social form of Christ in the world today is considered: race, state and ethnicity. In each case there is something of immense value to be gained from the discussion. In the case of race, focusing on the one human race highlights the enormity of what Christians claim to have stumbled on in their interpretation of God in Christ. Though the truth-claims made border on the arrogant, they have to be made if they are relevant to humanity as a whole.

As far as the state is concerned, we are reminded that it is unwise to make any claim that Christ is embodied in what a state does or is. Nevertheless, there is a connection between decisions made by the state and the institutional social forms in which Christ is embodied (family, labour, church, marriage, friendships, culture) and this means that the concepts and realities of state, nation or government should not be detached from the concerns of theology.

Finally, the ethnicity of any presentation of Jesus the Christ is recognized as crucial in reflecting Jesus' particularity and reminding us of our own. No group can claim Christ for itself. Living 'in Christ' celebrates God in Christ's presence in the world, in particular social forms. But Christ challenges the idolization of any particular form. The celebration of the presence of God in human form is not the same as the worship of the human. Christ transcends particularity. Diversity is not thereby stifled. Christ's incorporation of diversity entails human groups' inclusion of those who may be radically different from each other, yet are nevertheless 'in Christ'.

All three sections in this chapter have left us at the same point. We must now examine in more detail the smaller, more localized, more concrete forms in which Christ may be deemed to be present in the world today. Over the next three chapters, then, attention will be turned to how Christ takes shape as a 'community of practice' (Chapter 4) in the worlds of work and education (Chapter 5) and in families/households, friendships and church (Chapter 6).

4 Christ as community of practice (I): A basic framework

Christian reflection in public

Some years ago, after over a decade teaching theology in higher education, I began a postgraduate degree in education. It was a part-time programme, undertaken mostly by distance learning, though containing one-to-one contact with a tutor and the option of group tutorials at a regional centre. Like many students, I found these group tutorials to be crucial to my enjoyment of the course. The tutorials also contributed to my understanding and use of the material presented, both through the content discussed, but also through the way they operated and the sometimes surprising exchanges which occurred and insights which cropped up.

In all three groups in which I was a participant I was the only one from the world of theology or religious studies. In every case, furthermore, I received no clue at all that any of the other participants belonged to a religious group of any kind. Nevertheless, being involved in these groups proved profoundly instructive for understanding more about the social forms in which Christ is present in the world today.

One feature stands out from my involvement. Time and again, as we discussed an aspect of recent theory or practice from the world of education ('narrative', 'culture', 'mind', 'learning organization', 'participation', 'community', 'formation'), usually in relation to school or college experience, a tutor or student would say to me: 'I don't suppose there are examples, though, from your involvement in church life.' I was in fact very easily translating aspects of the discussion into church examples, and constantly making direct links with recent developments in theology.

This illustrates how, despite much talk of inter-disciplinarity, so much learning remains compartmentalized. And yet it also shows that disciplines are not as self-contained as they might like to think. Disciplines and discourses are influenced from beyond themselves, whether they like it or not. Though disciplines have their own discourses and their own cultures, they are part of a larger environment ('society') which influences them, however much they may be seeking to influence it too.

Why 'church' might be good for you

There was one really striking occasion when people expressed surprise that, being involved in church life, I might already know something about the educational subject matter under discussion. This was during a module on education management. As I participated in the group I was drawing on past experience of working as a teacher and manager in college contexts, but my most immediate experience, in the post I was in at the time, was of managing groups and projects within the life of the church. The tutor – a school head teacher – praised me for an assignment I had written on a particular aspect of management. He was especially impressed at my awareness of 'real world issues' in my discussion of structures and behaviour in organizations. He admitted that he had not expected such awareness from someone working for the church.

Having established that he was not joking about his level of surprise, I accepted his invitation to try to spell out for the benefit of the whole group how and why I had been able to write as I did. Two insights surfaced immediately from what I said and, importantly, from the all-too-brief discussion that followed. The first insight resulted from the simple fact that I had been in the church all my life, and whatever else the church might be, it is also a human organization. I have thus been involved in an organization, the membership of which I have little say in, and which displays plenty of examples of both success and failure (whether in roughly equal measure is difficult to say).

Second, the seemingly peculiar practice of churchgoing

confronts you on a regular basis with both the possibilities and the limitations of the human condition. To put it another way: living life consciously within the spirit of God, at its best, is utterly empowering. On the other hand, saying a prayer of confession every week reminds you that all is far from perfect and that you are caught up in that imperfection, and always will be so long as you live on the earth.

I shall not forget the shock of seeing a group of well-educated professionals open-mouthed at reaching the fresh insight that Christianity might actually connect with 'real life'. And given that there are a great number of occasions when I, like many others, find myself asking 'Is all this church thing really worth it?', it was also a sobering, even uplifting, event for me. Being in churches can do more to you *positively* than you often think.[1]

The breadth of Christian living

However, I can see that a number of other observations need to be made. First, though I might speak about 'being in the church all my life' or about 'churchgoing' this is clearly shorthand for something more complex. My words veil the fact that 'just being there' or 'just going' are inadequate to describe what is contained in the notion of 'being in the church'. I need to own up also to the impact of a variety of forms of Christian family life, the support and stimulus of many different Christian friends, and to multiple experiences (good and bad) of church groups – house-groups, study groups, committees, working parties, retreats, 'awaydays' and conferences. I must also recognize the significance for me of seven years' formal study (of the Bible and Christian theology), and of being a trained, authorized preacher in the Christian denomination to which I belong (the Methodist Church). At issue, then, is what we must call the 'formation' of a Christian person. Churchgoers may well experience what confession is meant to achieve in the context of worship. But without a connection between worship and the rest of life, Christian faith can scarcely be considered a 'way of life'. Confession is thus to be seen as one element in a complex process of 'person-formation', which

---

[1] In saying this I do not, of course, want to deny that church involvement can also be very damaging too. But that particular discussion must be for another time.

includes worship and much more besides (e.g. private prayer, study, scripture-reading, charitable giving, political action).

The context in which the incident I am exploring here occurred leads to a second observation. This was a small group. We met only half a dozen times, for two hours at a time. I hardly knew anything about the people I was with. (This counted after all as a 'professional setting', even if it was all quite relaxed.) Yet it was still an encounter between people who were prepared not simply to remain in their heads when interacting. They talked about their life experience and their struggles of their working lives while wrestling with the theory being discussed in the module studied. Though there was tough cognitive stuff that had to be understood, analysed and discussed, people were able to say what they found difficult, and own up to the emotions they felt, as well as indicating what they thought.

Of course, it is important not to over-dramatize. These were short-lived groups. They were not therapy groups, even if there may have been a therapeutic element as people shared and wrestled with difficult aspects of their working life in the company of others in similar situations. Professional development at its best does, after all, develop the whole person. It does not just train someone in a skill, or feed them more cognitive knowledge. And I would not want to pretend for a moment that these groups did or could function *for all* as crucial contexts for 'person-forming', even if I personally found this particular group experience very enriching. Indeed, to get the most from groups, and for them to be person-forming in any sense, you have to be prepared to participate actively and often quite personally.[2] Nevertheless, the experience I describe serves as a reminder of the potential significance of small groups in human life, whatever form they take. It serves also as an ideal introduction to the subject matter of this and the next chapter.

The experience and reflection just described thus raise the question of the relationship and distinction between churchgoing and person-formation. The former is a social practice which can

---

[2] And accepting the fact that there are often contributors in small-group settings who misread this aspect of group interaction, or behave inappropriately, in seeking to dominate groups with their own stories, rather than using their experience in the cause of their and others' personal development.

contribute to the latter. The latter may include churchgoing, though clearly includes much more, even for Christians. In Christian understanding, however, the formation of persons will occur 'in Christ'. This will include some form of explicit relationship to a body of people who actively seek to be 'in Christ'. The challenge emerging from this present enquiry, however, is to explore how what it means to be 'in Christ' extends beyond 'church' because Christ appears to take social forms which are not simply to be identified with, and as, church. It is clear that if the significance of the experience I have narrated relates to what occurs in the context of encounter between people meeting in small groups, then I must explore further what is entailed. How might Christ be evident in any high-quality group encounter? It is at this point that Christian theology's role in amplifying how person-formation occurs in the context of the social interactions of everyday human living comes to the fore. I have become convinced that it is best to speak of this whole process as being 'formed as a person in and through Christ'. Furthermore, one of the terms which my work on education has introduced me to – 'community of practice' – provides a highly instructive concept with which to work to explore this process further. I am also convinced that it would be quite damaging to study the concept of 'community of practice' solely in relation to the human communities we call 'church'. God in Christ takes social form, and if God is active in the world, then this includes both the social form of church and other forms of social interaction. It is these other forms which it is practical theology's task to disclose and explore.

Working conclusions

These conclusions produce very obvious, but telling, consequences. First, it is not churchgoing alone that produces a Christian. Second, any groups in which people participate intensively may be contexts for disclosure of the presence of Christ. Persons are formed through their involvement in lots of groups. If people are, in Christian understanding, formed 'in Christ', then this means that participation in a whole variety of groups may prove to be participation in Christ. Third, it would be theologically disastrous to fail to support the christological exploration of what is already happening in the group contexts in and through which the formation of persons is occurring. Christian theology would be incomplete through being inadequately resourced by contemporary experience of Christ. And public discussion of what it means to be human would be inadequately resourced theologically. Fourth, experience *and* reflection both need to occur for us to move towards being fully formed in Christ. It was only as a result of the interaction within the group that the stimulus for my own reflection occurred, and it was only in the light of further reflection that the above observations came to light. Churches also need to be contexts within which such reflection can happen. Even if they can be, however, they may not necessarily be the best place for such reflection, for all people at all times.[3] Fifth, for the individual, some kind of 'running commentary' on life is needed for a person to be able to undertake reflection on their process of growth (in Christian terms, their continual formation in Christ).[4] In more traditional terms, we might want to say that a person's devotional or worshipping/liturgical life is essential. This is true. But as I shall demonstrate over the next two chapters, it is too easy to make quick assumptions about what phrases such as 'devotional or worshipping/liturgical life' mean. There may, in fact, be many ways of resourcing a theologically informed 'running commentary'. And at a time when 'fresh expressions of church' are 'emerging' all the time,[5] we need to be careful that we

---

[3] I am drawing here on my experience of what actually happens in the context of formal theological education (in 'academic contexts': college or course settings), where profound insights, personal learning and spiritual development often occur.

[4] Most recently I have begun to use the image of 'soundtrack' to try and enable people to grasp how theology works. A theological tradition is like a soundtrack in that it accompanies and interprets a life. But in the same way that a soundtrack is not only words (but always a combination of dialogue, sounds and music), a theological tradition is more than a 'cognitive resource'. Soundtracks sometimes jar with what is on screen. They sometimes do not 'work' for all viewers. They are also manipulative at times. They offer emotional support. I hope to develop the use of this image for theology further in due course.

[5] This discussion links with the now widespread exploration of 'new ways of being church' and, to use more recent terminology, 'fresh expressions of church' and 'emerging church'. A good example of such material can be found in the writings of Brian McLaren, one of whose recent titles, *A Generous Orthodoxy*, Grand Rapids: Zondervan, 2004, provides the helpful reminder that elements in the 'new' are sometimes very old. The emerging church movement has, however, tapped into the sense that existing churches (buildings and people) can be very alien environments for those not used to religion or spirituality of any kind.

do not assume in advance how person-formation in and through Christ inevitably must occur.

But I am running ahead of myself. I must first establish that it is at all appropriate and helpful to speak of Christ as a 'community of practice', and demonstrate how such a strategy might contribute to an understanding of how persons are formed in and through Christ.

Christ and the concept of 'community of practice'

Christ as a 'community of practice' sounds bizarre. For, in Christian understanding, is it not the single, historical figure of Jesus who is the Christ? And does not the apparent switch of focus onto a group of human beings undermine the sense that, when we have to do with Jesus, we have to do with God? Have we not succumbed to the temptation of anthropocentrism, and started talking about human beings again?[6]

Yet saying that 'Christ is a community of practice' is only as bizarre as telling a group of early Christians that 'you are the body of Christ' (the apostle Paul, in 1 Cor. 12.27) or speaking of 'Christ existing as community' (Dietrich Bonhoeffer). Throughout this book and its predecessor, *Christ in Focus*, I have sought to demonstrate how important it is *not* to let the figure of Jesus become isolated, and *not* to view the saviour figure individualistically. This insight applies both at the point of Christianity's origin and when Jesus the saviour is received and interpreted in the contexts and communities of later Christian history.

In order to develop an understanding of Christ as a community of practice, I have chosen some conversation partners who may seem somewhat surprising: social and educational theorists, social psychologists and, especially, management consultants. But there should not be much surprise about the approach I am adopting. Truth is truth wherever it is found, and my enquiries throughout have been based on the theological premise conveyed in Bonhoeffer's insight that 'it is only by living completely in the world that one learns to have faith'.

---

[6] On anthropocentrism as a distortion of Christocentrism in Christian theology, see *Christ in Focus*, pp. 53–4.

'Community of practice': a working definition

What is meant by 'community of practice'? And why is this a useful concept in trying to clarify who and where Christ is, and what social form Christ takes? One basic working definition comes from Wenger, McDermott and Snyder:

> Communities of practice are groups of people who share a concern, a set of problems, or a passion about a topic, and who deepen their knowledge and expertise in this area by interacting on an ongoing basis.[7]

What do they do? In business terms,

> Communities of practice connect people from different organizations as well as across independent business units. In the process, they knit the whole system together around core knowledge requirements . . . [As such, they] are the ideal social structure for 'stewarding' knowledge.[8]

It is important to understand that the 'knowledge' that Wenger, McDermott and Snyder are referring to is not the mere acquisition of cognitively processed data propositions. Knowledge incorporates practice and experience ('knowing how'). It also entails making explicit what often remains hidden. By making the implicit explicit, 'knowers' can develop through reflection on their practice, and others can benefit from their skills and awareness. Knowledge is social (held and developed by groups[9]) and dynamic. And according to Wenger, McDermott and Snyder, cultivating communities of practice within an organization is an art.[10]

Such language and concepts are pertinent both to theological reflection and to Christian living. The most obvious links are with what it means to be 'church'. However, exploration of what it means for any human group to be a 'community of practice' can

---

[7] E. Wenger, R. McDermott and W. M. Snyder, *Cultivating Communities of Practice*, Boston, Mass.: Harvard Business School Press, 2002, p. 4.

[8] Wenger, McDermott and Snyder, *Cultivating*, pp. 6 and 12.

[9] 'Though our experience of knowing is individual, knowledge is not' (Wenger, McDermott and Snyder, *Cultivating*, p. 10).

[10] Wenger, McDermott and Snyder, *Cultivating*, p. 14.

prove instructive for thinking about social forms of Christ in other contexts too.[11]

I shall examine the usefulness of the concept of 'community of practice' with respect to 'church' more fully in Chapter 6, and draw out the full practical potential of the concept in Chapter 7. At this point, I need only point out some main features of the concept which suggest that it might be fruitful to link certain social forms of life with participation in Christ.

'Communities of practice': what do they achieve?

Communities of practice are groups which contain and generate energy. Because they form in relation to a common concern or purpose, then members bring drive and commitment with them.

Second, communities of practice are interactive. Through operating in this way they bring the best out of their members. They promote give-and-take among their members in a way that resists inappropriate competitiveness between them. Each member knows that all benefit from the way that people contribute differently at different times, taking a lead or holding back as appropriate.

Third, communities of practice 'grow out of practice'. They 'cannot be managed into existence'.[12] In other words, people already engaged in the task around which the community of practice forms are the ones who will become its members.

Fourth, communities of practice meet when they need to meet, in forms appropriate to their task. Their members have a strong sense of belonging, as co-workers in an identifiable area of work, and are in connection with each other in a variety of ways. They call or email each other if they have no face-to-face meeting planned, though recognize the immense value of embodied, rather than merely virtual, meeting.

Fifth, communities of practice are communities, not networks.

---

[11] Ultimately, such practice could be called 'practising the presence of Christ', so long as this is not turned into a sense that human activity can somehow of itself 'summon up' Christ's presence. Practice of the presence of Christ remains the discovery of a gift.

[12] D. Cohen and L. Prusak, *In Good Company*, Boston, Mass.: Harvard Business School Press, 2001, p. 22.

In other words, a notion of insiders and outsiders is at work. There may well be overlap between members of a community of practice and networkers (members of such communities are often networkers themselves, as they seek new, appropriate knowledge in order better to address the task in hand), but membership has meaning. Those who participate in a particular community of practice are identifiably committed to it.

Sixth, among the greatest values of communities of practice is that they bring outcomes additional to their main purpose: for example, good relationships, a sense of belonging and identity, confidence, a spirit of inquiry.[13]

Communities of practice as forms of Christ

Now a link may be determinable between all of these six points and the church as a social body. But what of Christ? Why should a link be forged between Christ and these features of a community of practice? My contention is that, by referring to the concept of community of practice, we gain a better understanding of the contexts in which 'person-formation' occurs in human life. In turn, if we see these contexts in the light of Christ understood as a community of practice, then we gain fresh insight both into where and who Christ is today and into ways in which the institutional forms of life that we examine might be transformed by reference to Christ.

The six points just made can all be expressed in christological terms. First, Christ is experienced in the context of any group as an energizing power. God the Spirit, as known in and through Christ, is at work wherever human beings commit themselves to a common purpose which brings the best out of people, especially in the service of others.

Second, Christ is present in and through the way that people relate to each other, bringing out more than merely the sum of what individuals bring.

Third, Christ is already present in any people who are engaged in the work of bringing the best out of others. This form of Christ's presence is nothing other than God at work in the development of

---

[13] Wenger, McDermott and Snyder, *Cultivating*, p. 15.

human beings towards the purpose that God intends for all creation. Whenever groups form which are focused upon human well-being and development, and which stretch and draw out their participants as they contribute to human flourishing, then the presence of God in Christ is becoming evident.

Fourth, people remain 'in Christ' whether they are physically together or not. Those who consciously follow Christ know that they need to meet others face to face at regular intervals. But their sense of belonging and purpose – their being formed in Christ, and participating in Christ in whatever groups they belong to – exists for them as individuals.

Fifth, the institutional contexts which I shall examine through the 'community of practice' lens are usually clear about their boundaries. Similarly, it is usually clear on the part of the followers of Jesus Christ who wants to be included and who does not. The challenge of this aspect of Christ as community of practice, however, is to assess the value, if any, of talking about boundaries and boundary-crossing *at all* with respect to Christ. There will clearly be points of tension as we examine the capacity of the groups and institutional contexts under scrutiny (work, education, families, friendships, church) to function as social forms of Christ. To take an example: a family may function as a primary context for the formation of persons. But for a family or a household to be seen as a social form of Christ will mean being challenged in its exclusivity. If a family or household fails to prepare its members to relate outwards to others, then it has inadequately mirrored what it means to be a form of Christ. Seeing Christ as a community of practice thus questions any lazy identification of what it means for Christ being 'for all'. The tough reality of the way that human groups actually work is respected when it is recognized that Christ takes many social forms. Christ 'for all' does not, however, mean that the challenges of living in real, social groups can be overlooked. The challenge of Christ thus entails respect for social boundaries, while acknowledging at the same time that Christ stretches the boundaries of human communities and ensures that they are not fixed but porous.

Sixth, respecting Christ as a community of practice means acknowledging the multi-dimensional way in which Christ enables human fulfilment to occur. People are enriched through

Christ's presence, and enriched all the more through consciousness of that presence.

Three things are, however, *not* being claimed through this interpretation of Christ by reference to the concept of community of
practice. First, I am not claiming that any and every human group
is a community of practice. Second, I am not claiming that every
community of practice is inevitably a form of Christ. Not all social
groups, after all, are healthy for society.[14] Third, I am not claiming
that all communities of practice that foster human well-being
intentionally seek to participate in Christ. Though I am claiming
that Christ is at work in all such groups, this is a Christian interpretation of what is happening. This reading of Christ in relation
to the concept of 'community of practice' is offered with the intention of urging that greater attention be paid to human transformation. But it is precisely that: a 'way of reading' (a means of
theological reflection) in the service of what groups and relationships can, at their best, achieve. Theology, however, pushes a
group beyond itself to ask how a group or relationship is
resourced for what it can do to those who participate in it. To speak
of 'Christ' is not, then, simply another term for what a group does.

Conclusions

What can be distilled from all of this? I am beginning from the
theological premise that God wills the best for all God's creatures.
God wants all in creation to flourish, and none to suffer unjustly.
The relative freedom in which the created order operates does,
however, mean that flourishing and the resisting of evil and suffering are difficult to achieve. As far as the human component of
creation is concerned, the divine project is the creation of persons:
people who relate to each other in a way befitting God's will for
the world. God's will for the world is that the reign of God comes
into being. Human beings are seeking to be what they can yet be,
before God, in the future.[15]

---

[14] F. Fukuyama, *The Great Disruption: Human Nature and the Reconstitution of Social
Order*, London: Profile Books, 1999, p. 22; Cohen and Prusak, *In Good Company*,
pp. 56 and 77.
[15] Or, to express this in more technical language, theological anthropology has, at
root, to do with eschatology.

In Christian understanding, human participation in the divine project of creation entails being shaped 'in Christ'. Human beings have the opportunity to become persons by participating actively in forms of human community where Christ takes form in the world. Phrases such as 'being Christ-like' and 'imitating Christ' suggest individual endeavour in order to become like Jesus the individual. In contrast to this, the idea of Christ being present in social forms emphasizes that the formation of persons is both individual and communal. It is in Christ that God is undertaking the formation of human persons.

Once we turn our attention to the formation of human persons within the social forms in which Christ can be seen to be present in the world today, then we are compelled to pay attention to all formative social groups. Where are persons formed? How are they formed, across a whole variety of groups in which people are involved? This is where the value of the concept of 'communities of practice' becomes clear. Rather than concentrate on the human individual, the individual Christian believer, or the church alone, it is imperative that Christian theology examine christologically the human groups in which people are actively becoming persons. These are 'communities of practice' – 'Communities of practice are everywhere. We all belong to a number of them.'[16] Whether or not something as grand as 'human flourishing' or 'the formation of persons' is the purpose for a community of practice's existence, human flourishing is at the very least a by-product in the social contexts to be examined in the next two chapters. In the case of some, it stands at the forefront. The formation of a person 'in Christ' can, theologically speaking, be seen as one of the 'intangible outcomes' that writers on communities of practice describe as inevitable when a community works well.

In Christian perspective, then, close attention to what happens in the communities of practice to which we belong (be they family, friendships, work, leisure group, education or church) will enrich human understanding of the formation of persons. Explorations of such relationships and groups should not be seen as 'applied Christology'. It is, rather, 'Christology in reverse',

---

[16] Wenger, McDermott and Snyder, *Cultivating*, p. 5.

whereby we work back from the social forms in which Christ is perceived to be present today to what can be said of Christ. We are, in other words, working at the 'experience' end of the theological spectrum – but resisting the notion that Christology is simply spun out of experience. For experience and tradition remain in the closest possible interaction as we proceed. God in Christ may have some surprises in store. But we must expect that God will remain recognizable as the God we have already known in Christ, as we discover more about who God in Christ is, and what God in Christ is doing in the task of person-forming today.[17]

---

[17] It may have struck some readers that I could have conducted most of the discussion in this chapter thus far with reference to a different fashionable concept – 'social capital'. Christ could have been deemed to be, or at least to have drawn upon, the 'social glue' on which all successful communities depend. (For more on the concept, see e.g. F. Fukuyama, *Trust: The Social Virtues and the Creation of Prosperity*, London: Penguin, 1996, *passim*; Cohen and Prusak, *In Good Company*; and for discussion in a theological context, A. Morisy, *Journeying Out: A New Approach to Christian Mission*, London, New York and Harrisburg: Morehouse, 2004, esp. ch. 3.) I chose not to do so for one main reason: social capital is a more abstract concept. Admittedly, Morisy's use of the concept is profoundly engaged and concrete. Use of the term 'social capital' need not, therefore, tend in the direction I fear. And 'community' is a far from unproblematic concept. But at least it forces an interpreter to think in concrete terms about what forms 'Christ as community' might take.

5 Christ as community of practice (II): Work and education

Christ at work

The meaning of work

It is a commonplace observation that most people 'derive a substantial part of their self-esteem from their work and work life'.[1] I would take it further. A great many people appear to derive a great sense of their worth as persons from who they are and what they achieve in the context of work. Here, of course, 'work' usually means paid employment. Money continues to talk, even though, for those who have fulfilling paid work, the money may matter less than the sense of value and the enjoyment experienced in the work itself.

'Work' may, though, mean any regular, purposeful, meaningful activity, especially when it involves an impact on others, be it paid or not. Huge amounts of 'domestic work' are unpaid and unnoticed. Yet it is vital, and often fulfilling. Gone are the days when a contestant on a TV game-show introducing herself as a 'housewife' would be greeted with a loud round of applause and a patronizing comment from the host. But we are still far from considering the work of a househusband, housewife or other domestic carer as similar in value to that, say, of a regional sales manager, social worker, university lecturer or shop-owner. Unpaid voluntary work in the community may be well regarded – especially when undertaken by people with professional skills who donate their time alongside or beyond long,

[1] D. Cohen and L. Prusak, *In Good Company*, Boston, Mass.: Harvard Business School Press, 2001, p. 49.

busy well-paid working lives – but, in other cases, much voluntary work or domestic work remains less socially valued. This
can and must continue to change as part of the ongoing transformation of Western societies. Viewing the contexts in which
all such work is undertaken from the perspective of christologically interpreted communities of practice can be part of that
transformation.

We must also note that there are hugely differing levels of sat-
isfaction in paid work. Cohen and Prusak remark:

> Although we ourselves sometimes fall into the trap of talking
> about 'employers' and 'employees' – the user and the used –
> those terms really belong to the industrial-age model and are
> inappropriate to the kinds of work and working relation-
> ships we consider here.[2]

This comment is important in a number of respects. As represen-
tatives of the wide world of research and writing on management and organizational issues, Cohen and Prusak reveal that
much of the writing is for managers. It is also produced out of
and for contexts where the information technology revolution
has taken full effect and where reflection on how organizations
work is heeded. It does not, in other words, fully account for
those who are still very much 'employees', on whom organization theory has had little impact, or who may be in small, finan-
cially vulnerable companies or organizations where survival and
making basic ends meet are pressing concerns.[3] There is, then, a
danger that in making theological use of the concept of 'community of practice' we may be setting out with a very rosy and
therefore unrealistic view of what might be possible in the world
of work and employment.

All of that said, work of all kinds is crucial for human well-
being. At its best, it contributes to person-formation for people at
all levels, through the relationships that are formed and fostered

---

[2] Cohen and Prusak, *In Good Company*, p. 17.
[3] In contributing to a recent church report which included theological reflection on
management literature, a reader commented that some of our observations
seemed 'dated'. Such 'datedness' appears more the case when one begins from
literature which reflects latest developments in organizational change. It appears
rather different from the perspective of pastoral work among those in employment at many levels in working life.

through it. If Christ is found in, or as, a community of practice in the world of work, the theological challenge is to explore further what it means to make such an identification. How can the patterns of living identified in Chapter 2 take shape in the world of work? In particular, how can such patterns take shape when the world of work for most people is by definition built on some form of 'master–slave' relationship?

Groups at work

A community of practice capable of being person-forming may occur in any kind of work context. It is not the position in an organizational structure or the status or rank of members of a working group or team (be that similar to each other or different) which determines whether or not the group will function as a person-forming community of practice. Rather, this is determined by the willingness of the people to work with each other and learn from each other. ('An effective community of practice offers a place of exploration where it is safe to speak the truth and ask hard questions.'[4]) One may, of course, learn much as a member of a work group or team. But whether it functions formatively beyond its role of simply enabling a person to do the job depends on how open people can be with each other.

I stress that I am not arguing that every group one belongs to becomes some sort of support or therapy group. In the context of work, after all, the primary reason why groups exist is to get jobs done. I am, however, respecting a crucial insight of research into communities of practice – the 'intangible outcomes' of belonging mean that more happens for members than the mere doing of the job. I am also focusing on the fact that person-formation happens in many social contexts, and not always in intentional ways.

Admittedly, a 'communities of practice' approach to the value of work stresses the positive achievements of people working in groups. Furthermore, communities of practice may include

[4] E. Wenger, R. McDermott and W. M. Snyder, *Cultivating Communties of Practice*, Boston, Mass.: Harvard Business School Press, 2002, p. 37.

people working at different levels within an organization.[5] At their best they enable fruitful interaction between people of different status, and working at different levels. But it would be foolish to overlook the fact that level, rank or status usually does carry significance in the employment world and that human interaction is often obstructed by the different roles that people play. We need to recognize the lingering impact of a master–slave mentality in work.

The master–slave mentality

This mentality needs to be examined, not simply because of its New Testament use, but also because to dodge it is to overlook the way that working contexts are often actually *experienced* by people in them. ('Who was your slave last?' 'She's a real slave-driver, she is.' These examples of workplace banter reveal much.) At root, wherever one person has the power to require that another does something that they might otherwise choose not to do, then a basic dynamic in human relations is set up. We may refer to it by many different names (employer–employee, man-ager–co-worker, supervisor–assistant). But a fundamental power relation exists which cannot be escaped. This basic dynamic must be addressed if grand ideas about Christ being socially formed in the context of people's working relationships are to carry weight.

A number of observations are important. First, Christ can take social form in working life *in spite of* whatever role relationships exist. If a supervisor helps a supervisee, or a manager a team member, then even if their roles as supervisor or manager are important in each case, it is never by virtue of the role alone that

[5] It is here where, ironically, a communities of practice approach admittedly ducks a complex aspect of working life. Though members of a community of practice may indeed work at different levels within the hierarchy of an organization, the point about communities of practice is that the rank of members is relativized because the community to which they belong forms around a common purpose or task. In comparative terms in the life of a church, it is like members having to make decisions in a church council (when the voice of a priest/presbyter and office-holders in a church might carry greater weight by virtue of role), as dis-tinguished from the same members being part of an ecumenical fellowship/ study group structure which they do not lead, yet which exists for members' spiritual support.

God in Christ is at work.[6] Christ is not 'more present' in a manager or supervisor; they grow as people too in the interactions that occur.[7]

Second, we must banish any lazy theology of 'servant leadership' which over-romanticizes the gospel texts and makes an easy appeal to the example of Jesus in the context of working life.[8] The canonical Gospels certainly present some crucial motifs and insights related to the figure of Jesus which form part of God in Christ's challenge to all forms of human relationship, including those in the world of work. However, there is a major difficulty in simply 'applying' readings of gospel texts, and imagining on the basis of these readings that Jesus 'must have' been the best of all possible managers. Such an approach to the use of the Gospels seems to me misguided. For such a procedure may simply be heard as saying that Jesus, the first-century Palestinian peasant, would inevitably make the best sort of office manager or corporate director: it is just a matter of adopting his style, and all will be well. This is clearly absurd. What, though, do we learn from reconsidering master–slave imagery through a christological lens?

The first point to address is that the master–slave dynamic is deeply prevalent in all forms of working life, paid and voluntary. All readers will have known or been people who thrived on being able to say to one person '"Go," and he goes, and to another, "Come," and he comes,' or '"Do this", and he does it' (Matt. 8.9). Likewise, all readers will have known or been people who have received legitimate working instructions with great reluctance and proved obstructive to the smooth running of a project or organi-

---

[6] That is, even if it is by virtue of the fact that their tasks of supervision and management are what sensitive supervisors and managers can use to aid the personal development of supervisees and employees.

[7] It would be invidious to speak of 'degrees of growth'. Furthermore, to think of work teams and working relationships in terms of 'communities of practice' encourages a movement away from measurement of achievement towards collectively enabled qualitative growth of persons.

[8] Some attempts to do this are better than others, of course! John Adair is an example of someone who has written for a church readership about leadership in the church, but has also introduced reference to the example of Jesus into mainstream management literature. See, for example, John Adair, *Effective Leadership: A Modern Guide to Developing Leadership Skills*, London and Sydney: Pan Books, 1983, and *The Leadership of Jesus*, Norwich: Canterbury Press, 2001.

zation. Such a 'command model' of working life is, of course, inevitable to some degree. Division of labour is necessary and roles and tasks are rightly allocated in accordance with training, skills and experience. But in work, what matters is how people handle their roles and relate to each other within them. Where there is more than professionalism, politeness or mere civility, and people relate with full respect for each other's human dignity, then that is the hallmark of a working team or group that can be seen as a community of practice in which Christ becomes present. If there is openness and mutual respect, then a community of practice can exist. Without this, there is no community and less possibility of Christ being embodied in the inter-relationship between those who work together. The body of Christ is fractured.[9]

A biblical passage which has proved telling in the history of Christian spirituality and ethical practice is Mark 10.35–45. This text finds the disciples disputing with each other as to who is the most important. James and John are cast in a bad light for wanting to claim special status within the group of disciples immediately around Jesus. In dealing with the other disciples' anger at James' and John's aspirations, Jesus explains how the way of relating that he commends is different from that of 'the Gentiles', whose rulers 'lord it over them' (Mark 10.42). By contrast, 'it is not so among you', for 'whoever wishes to become great among you must be your servant (*diakonos*), and whoever wishes to be first among you must be slave (*doulos*) of all' (Mark 10.43–44).

How is this text to be made use of in the world of work? In what ways is it instructive for understanding how Christ takes shape in the context of unequal relationships? Three observations can be made.

First, it is important to work back from the final verse of the text: 'For the Son of Man came not to be served but to serve, and to give his life a ransom for many' (Mark 10.45). Whether or not this saying derives from Jesus of Nazareth,[10] the verse indicates that Mark places the narrative in a christological and soteriologi-

---

[9] And the body of Christ *is*, and remains, fractured. It is also being healed, via resurrection. If this were not so, and Christians did not believe it, then there would be no faith, no church and no hope of God's coming reign.

[10] For discussion, see, for example, M. Hooker, *The Gospel According to St Mark*, London: A & C Black, 1991, pp. 247–51.

cal context. In other words, discussions about 'lording it over' take place in the context of what we know happened to Jesus himself. If anyone proves able to resist the desire to lord it over others, it is going to be a difficult path. In the same way that Jesus' actions in the service of others led to death, so those who follow him in resisting the desire to lord it over people are accepting the possibility of suffering. They have taken up their cross and are risking their lives (Mark 8.34–35).[11]

Second, we have to ask whether Jesus himself expects this way of operating to be very successful beyond the community of faith. He draws a simple contrast between the way that he and the disciples are to relate to each other as Jews, and the way in which others (the Gentiles) relate who are beyond the Jewish community of faith. By this, Mark may be suggesting that Jesus is fully aware of how limited his way of operating can be. It may have a chance of working within a community of faith, but it will not work outside it.

There is something in this insight. On the other hand, the reference to 'all' in Mark 10.44 and the phrase 'for many' in Mark 10.45 both stress that this is a way of operating that Jesus expects people to risk *beyond* a community of faith. In contemporary perspective, furthermore, such risk-taking is essential if religious groups are not to remain enclosed and their insights to make little impact on public life. So discussion of this text reminds readers of the difficulty of working with powerful theological insights in a world that may be unwilling to acknowledge their value.

The third observation is a direct consequence of the previous point and takes the form of a challenge. Does the teaching to be 'slaves of all' merely set up followers of Jesus to conduct themselves in an unrealistic way in wider society? Will they praise and cultivate weakness and servility, as Nietzsche accused Christians of doing, and therefore never prove effective leaders and managers without compromising or bracketing their

---

[11] In the context of the full Christian narrative about Jesus' life, death and resurrection, of course, it is also clear that the path being followed is ultimately believed to be a joyful (one resurrection awaits). Mark's narrative is, however, the most spartan of the canonical texts with regard to the resurrection and the ending of his Gospel ambiguous (see e.g. Hooker, *The Gospel According to St Mark*, pp. 388–94). Mark's emphasis is clearly on 'the way of the cross'.

Christian convictions in the world of work?[12] Will they therefore have to miss out on participating in Christ in the world of work?

This major objection is not easily met. I can see some substance to Nietzsche's critique of Christianity on this matter. Managers who happen to be Christians sometimes overcompensate for their faith in trying to demonstrate to colleagues without faith that they really can be ruthless when necessary. Or, more often, pastoral sensitivity to workers' whole situations and life contexts, and the desire not to lord it over others, result in gentle, caring leadership, even at the cost of getting a job done.

Rather than ultimately agree with Nietzsche, however, it seems better to me to interpret the Bible passage more in terms of the sheer enormity of its challenge for those who seek to live by it. It does not have to lead to weakness, to hyper- or over-sensitivity to the needs of others, or to an overbearing fear of offending or pressurizing others in the workplace. Rather, it challenges people in all forms of relationships not to lord it over others, even where they do have to make demands of them, and do have tasks to fulfil. It makes perfect sense to locate discussion of the passage from Mark in relation to working in a community of practice. As Cohen and Prusak note: 'Social capital . . . is not about being "nice".'[13] How, then, can you do what you have to do

---

[12] F. Nietzsche, *Human All Too Human*, Cambridge: Cambridge University Press, 1986 (German original 1878), ch. 3 'The Religious Life'.

[13] Cohen and Prusak, *In Good Company*, p. 13. There is an intriguing echo here with the oft-cited quotation from Stanley Hauerwas: 'American Methodism is surely only quite incidentally related to Christianity. (That is not to say that Methodists are without any convictions. Quite the contrary. For now that I am back among the Methodists, I have discovered that they do have a conviction: It is that God is nice. Moreover, since Methodists are a sanctificationist people, we have a correlative: We ought to be nice too. I must admit, one of the things that bothers me about Cobb's God is that she is just too damned nice!') – 'Knowing How to Go On When You Do Not Know Where You Are: A Response to John Cobb' in *Wilderness Wanderings*, Boulder and Oxford: Westview Press, 1997, pp. 25–31, here p. 29. Neither Cohen and Prusak's nor Hauerwas' quotation should, however, be used to justify being deliberately offensive! I observe at this point that I received a number of comments in response to the statement I made in *Christianity in a Post-Atheist Age*, London: SCM Press, 2002, that I did not think there was such a thing as a 'theology of politeness' (p. 91). I stand by the comment, where 'politeness' means a way of operating that merely observes social niceties for effect, without necessarily reflecting true respect for an Other. I do, of course, wholly support the notion that there is a theology of respect, and a theology of human dignity.

in the world of work, when tough things will undoubtedly arise, while keeping good relations and not demeaning those with whom you work at any point? That is the real challenge of the text. Only if that challenge is taken up can a Christian understanding of the master–slave metaphor have a chance of being viably useful. And only if a working context functions as a community of practice, in which the traces of Christ's presence mapped out in Chapter 2 begin to appear, can we then speak of Christ being present in social form. Being 'slave of all' does not mean, then, being servile in the process of resisting the tendency to 'lord it over' others.

Discussion of Paul's appropriation of the 'slave of all' tradition takes us a step further. Dale Martin's analysis of Paul's use of the slave language helps to show that his phrase 'slave to all' (1 Cor. 9.19) is more complex in meaning than has often been assumed in Christian discourse.[14] In his comprehensive and persuasive study *Slavery as Salvation: The Metaphor of Slavery in Pauline Christianity*, Martin shows how hearing the term 'slave' out of the context of the Greco-Roman world in which the New Testament emerged can lead contemporary readers to offer simplistic readings of Paul (slavery = a bad thing, without qualification). Reading relevant New Testament passages within the literature of the period shows up more subtle nuances implied in the texts.

Two features of Martin's study are especially important. In a first-century context, being a slave is not an inevitably negative image. Though 'most slaves probably held lowly, menial positions', some held a wide variety of positions in society, and there existed a hierarchy of slaves.[15] Indeed, 'slaves higher up in the hierarchy – management slaves – held a fair amount of power and influence relative both to the other slaves and to the society

---

[14] I am indebted to both Judith Lieu and Frances Young for drawing my attention to this important work.

[15] Dale B. Martin, *Slavery as Salvation: The Metaphor of Slavery in Pauline Christianity*, New Haven and London: Yale University Press, 1990, p. 15. Martin lists a great many jobs held by slaves: 'book publishing, business, clerical occupations, entertainment, medicine, teaching, philosophy . . . temple maintenance . . . constables and keepers of the peace . . . barbers, mirror makers, goldsmiths, cooks and architects . . . shopkeepers . . . craftspersons, fishermen, foremen, laborers, gladiators, personal servants, painters, and prostitutes' (p. 11). With the exception of gladiators (perhaps now replaced by professional footballers), the list reads like a contemporary list of jobs that people take up.

at large.'[16] Therefore, when Paul refers to himself as a 'slave of Christ' (Rom. 1.1; Gal. 1.10; Phil. 1.1),[17] the reference need not be heard as socially demeaning. This is the case despite the fact that Paul can still use slavery as a negative image elsewhere in his writings (e.g. Rom. 8.12–17, where 'enslavement to fear' is mentioned).

Second, being a slave can have a primary meaning of being linked to, and supported by, someone else. At the top end of the hierarchy of slaves, as Martin shows, slavery is part of a 'wider social structure of patron–client obligations and benefits'.[18] Dependence remains a fundamental feature of slave life. We are not talking here about redefining the top end of slavery as some kind of ancient middle class. The pieces of evidence that Martin surveys at one point in his discussion 'do not prove that slaves enjoyed wonderfully secure and happy home lives within the context of the nuclear family. Nor do they prove that the majority of slaves were able to maintain even a minimal family structure.'[19] The point is simply that we should hear Paul as saying that, as a slave of Christ, he has a good master and is well looked after. He has in fact 'gone up in the world' in being enslaved to Christ.[20] Being 'enslaved to Christ' could therefore be heard in a liberating way by slaves who aspired to rise up the hierarchy of slavery.

These observations of Martin's are important on so many fronts. They challenge, on historical-critical and literary grounds, the way in which the positively oriented slavery passages from the New Testament are so easily used in Christian practice. These texts have to be used cautiously, and with conscious awareness of the literary and historical context out of which they come. The 'positive use' (which entails the meaning 'being a slave can be OK') must be handled sensitively lest it lead to the psychologi-

---

[16] Martin, *Slavery as Salvation*, p. 15.

[17] And it is striking that in all three instances the NRSV translates *doulos* (*douloi* in Phil. 1.1, as Timothy is also referred to) as 'servant/s', with 'slave/s' being relegated to a footnote, as an alternative translation in each case.

[18] Martin, *Slavery as Salvation*, p. 25.

[19] Martin, *Slavery as Salvation*, p. 6. Martin is here using evidence from funerary inscriptions.

[20] Martin concludes that Paul was 'the upwardly mobile slave of Christ' (*Slavery as Salvation*, p. 149).

cally distorted use which has run through Christian history and has led to 'servant ministry' being about servility.

Martin's observations mean, however, that focus has to switch to discussion of 'association with' and 'well-being in relation to' the one to whom one is enslaved when such servant/slave passages are interpreted. 'Slave to all' does not mean at the beck and call of all, but prepared to be associated with anyone, and bound up with them in a search for the well-being of all. It is more akin to the idea expressed in 'rank me with whom you will' from the Methodist Church's Covenant Service than to the self-abasing servility which Nietzsche castigated Christianity for promoting.[21]

These insights are important in suggesting how the inevitable master–slave dynamic of the world of work can be understood and then, if not undermined, at least redefined in a more positive way. In the same way that the circumstances surrounding Paul's own paid work (his retention of his trade as a tent-maker) and his use of slave imagery were, in Martin's words' 'anything but simple',[22] so also exploring how Christ can come into being in social form in the context of the world of work remains problematic. A way forward is to examine the ways in which Christ can be seen as a community of practice wherever groups and teams exist that foster human flourishing. When any social context in the world of work brings together people who work in a way that respects people's dignity and development, then God in Christ is clearly at work too.

Christ thus takes form as a community of practice working towards the fulfilment of God's eschatological project: the whole of creation under God's reign. The presence of a master–slave dynamic in the world of work means, however, that participation in Christ can prove to be profoundly difficult in a work setting. On certain understandings of Paul, furthermore, acceptance of the 'way things are' in the world may seem to be

[21] Allowing for the fact that there is undoubtedly a slightly paternalistic tone to the Covenant Prayer at this point, as perhaps could only be expected given the social background of the Wesleys. For the full text of the prayer (old and new forms), see *Methodist Worship Book*, Peterborough: Methodist Publishing House, 1999, p. 290. The new form of the prayer replaces the cited words with 'wherever you may place me' (p. 288).

[22] Martin, *Slavery as Salvation*, p. 149.

the way forward, as if things should simply be 'let be', even if they are unjust. But I have sought to offer ways of using the Gospel of Mark and Paul with a realism about the world of work.

Paul can seem very radical at one moment and socially and politically conservative at the next.[23] However, exploration of his use of slave imagery evokes sympathy for his dilemma: how could he handle and develop the theological traditions with which he worked, and enable them to be used transformatively, without changing the world first? Paul does not always expect slaves to seek freedom or be set free (1 Cor. 7.21). He did not ask Philemon to release Onesimus (Philemon 15–16). He can say there is neither slave nor free in Christ (Gal. 3.28), though accepts that slavery will remain. We find it easy to be critical of his conservatism. I am, though, conscious that, today, those who write about work and its rich possibilities are rarely those who experience work as drudgery. We *do* have to work with the world as it is, even while trying to change it.

To conclude this section: not every working relationship can be a community of practice. Christ may therefore struggle to find social form in the world of work. But work, at its best and in sometimes unlikely forms and contexts, can help people to flourish. It is not only high-level managers (or slaves) who might be stretched positively and blossom through their work. The respect for the value of ordinary work which followed the Reformation has sometimes produced patronizing comment.[24] But any job can be developmental and 'more than a job'. All working relations are contexts for graceful interaction. Honesty, forgiveness, repentance and amendment of life are crucial to a good and productive working environment. Stretching of one's own abilities, and encouragement of others to do likewise, in the

---

[23] For an example of the latter, see my article '"Who are you for?" I Cor. 1.10–17 as Christian scripture in the context of diverse methods of reading' in T. J. Burke and J. K. Elliott (eds), *Paul and the Corinthians*, Leiden: Brill, 2003, pp. 157–76.

[24] The good intentions of Martin Luther or George Herbert whose line 'A servant with this clause / Makes drudgery divine; / Who sweeps a room, as for thy laws, / Makes that and the action fine', (verse 4 of the hymn 'Teach me, my God and King') can too easily become the company director's plainly untrue statement that 'the cleaner is as important an employee in this business as I am'.

context of a safe working environment, is part of what it means to be 'in Christ'.[25]

Education into Christ

I have a vivid memory of a church planning meeting at which someone remarked that, because I was employed in higher education, I did not, in fact, know much about work in the 'real world'. Though fuming inwardly, I took the point, even though the speaker clearly knew very little about the financial pressures on educational institutions, the need to be income-generating, and the expansion of a business ethos throughout the education sector. While there is a difference between being a professional educator and being a student, there remains a true sense in which all who are involved in education are co-learners. And as any teacher or tutor will admit, on good days, being involved in education does not feel like work at all.

The experience of those 'good days' makes it possible to speak of the 'spirituality of education'. As one recent writer has expressed it:

> Practices of attentiveness, critical reflection and discernment with regard to creation, society and culture are recognisable features of good education. Such practices help to constitute more contemplative, deliberative and socially conscious selves. When educators incorporate these practices intentionally into pedagogical processes, they advance the spiritual dimension of life.[26]

From this generalized description of the potential of education to be person-forming it is not a huge step to a more particularly

---

[25] It is right to say quickly that contexts are best when they are 'non-judgemental'. This is true where 'non-judgemental' means not demeaning of people. Sometimes, however, non-judgemental has come to mean 'non-evaluative'. This is especially so in church life, where there is often a profound fear of any kind of critical appraisal of pieces of work undertaken or of work performance by those in paid or voluntary posts. It does, however, seem to me that rather than seeking to catch up on good practice throughout society, churches should be at the forefront of a willingness to appraise. Christian workers should know how to be able to give and receive appropriate criticism in the context of building people up (1 Cor. 14.26).

[26] C. M. Griffith, 'Education and Spirituality', *New Dictionary of Christian Spirituality*, London: SCM Press, 2005, p. 266.

Christian theological interpretation of what happens in educational contexts. Educational groups can be communities of practice in which Christ can be seen to take social form, along the lines of the patterns of life identified in Chapter 2.

What, though, makes educational groups any different from the groups at work already described in this chapter? Certainly there are many similarities, and some of the same limitations are present. There may not be a master–slave dynamic, but a teacher–pupil or tutor–student dynamic is present which can sometimes be a hindrance rather than a help to learning. This is especially so in the case of tutors and students in adult education contexts.[27] Nevertheless, there are particular features and forms of educational groups which are worth separate examination.[28] I shall present nine observations, all of which I suggest are pertinent to our christological enquiry.

First, there is an *intentionality* in educational groups which is not necessarily present in communities of practice in the world of work. In many educational contexts participants want to be there and are keen to learn.[29] By contrast, at work, though communities of practice form around tasks and responsibilities, there may be less drive explicitly to learn, or to be attentive to the impact of learning gained for the process of developing as a person. It is more possible in a working context to remain task-oriented, whereas in education what is happening to the person being educated is usually deemed important too.

Second, attention should be given to the christological significance of *what the word 'education' actually means*. *E-ducere* (the Latin form) means 'to lead out'. Educators, then, are seeking

---

[27] Though adult education is able to promote the view that all are co-learners more easily than is possible in many school contexts, it remains true that adults also want to know that their tutors are, if not 'experts', at least well qualified and knowledgeable in their field. This can sometimes lead to students regressing in their expectations of what tutors can and should do in shaping the educational environment, and to tutors either being unwilling to embrace their responsibility as leaders in the educational experience, or being forced (whether willingly or unwillingly) into an 'expert' role.

[28] I must emphasize that I am not here talking only, of course, about theological education. Settings in which theological exploration is explicit merely accentuates the relevance of what is to follow.

[29] School teachers will quickly and rightly say this is very often not the case in schools. I shall comment on this in the 'Critical postscript' below.

to draw out from those they teach what lies within. Education is about enabling people to discover what they are capable of, as they begin to discover who they are and what they know.

Admittedly, this approach to education is sometimes stretched to breaking point. The laws of aerodynamics, for example, have first to be 'got into' a person before they can be drawn back out again and used to design an aeroplane. Some aspects of knowledge do have to be 'banked' – in all disciplines. But the shift from banked knowledge to the process of knowing is important. And recognizing that learning is an active process which depends on drawing out what lies within the learner is of crucial importance. It becomes still more significant when education is considered through a christological lens. Christ is already there, available to the learner in the form of a new humanity waiting to be discovered in the human interactions that occur in any group that functions as a person-forming community of practice. Attention to the derivation of the word 'education' as 'leading out' thus enables emphasis to be placed on the fact that it is God's work in Christ which can be drawn out of learners.

The significance of *interaction in a learning group* – between *all* participants – is the third observation to be made. Again we are dealing with a fashionable catchword: inter-subjectivity.[30] Although education draws out what is within a person, what is discovered in a group context is always more for the individual group participant than what lies within any individual present. This is once more of crucial christological significance.[31] For if Christ is present in social form in contexts where person-formation is an 'intangible outcome', then the social form of that presence becomes especially clear in an educational setting. Christ needs the group in order to be present. Christ is more than any life-changing, transforming, spiritual power experienced by an individual. Christ is more than the sum of any such experiences

---

[30] This point, too, will be developed further in Chapter 7.

[31] This is, I think, a version of the point being made by Daniel Hardy when distinguishing 'society' from 'inter-subjectivity', where the latter allows individuals ultimately to remain detached from each other in their individuality (in 'Created and Redeemed Sociality' in C. Gunton and D. W. Hardy (eds), *On Being the Church: Essays on the Christian Community*, Edinburgh: T & T Clark, 1989, pp. 21–47, reprinted in D. W. Hardy, *God's Ways with the World: Thinking and Practising Christian Faith*, Edinburgh: T & T Clark, 1996, pp. 188–205).

drawn out in an educational context. Christ is experienced as per-son-forming in the context of a group process. This observation can pertain regardless of the subject matter of a group.[32] Engineers, linguists, sociologists, biologists, sports studies stu-dents – at whatever level they study – all have their own individ-ual work to do. But all receive more through collaborative endeavour because they learn about group interaction in the process of undertaking their work.

The way in which people come to participate in such educational groups is therefore, fourth, of relevance too. In educational circles in recent years Jean Lave's and Etienne Wenger's work on 'legiti-mate peripheral participation' (LPP) has proved widely influen-tial.[33] In their studies of how people in different trades and work contexts come to develop expertise in their professions, Lave and Wenger have observed that they become increasingly involved in the groups (communities of practice) in which they are likely to learn more about their trades. It does, however, take time to develop skills. This is less, then, a matter of undertaking an apprenticeship than of continual, increasing involvement in prac-tice within a group setting. Wenger reflects on the development of the concept:

> The term [LPP] is a bit unwieldy, but it does capture impor-tant conditions under which people can become members of a community of practice. We wanted to point out that the required learning takes place not so much through the reification of a curriculum as through modified forms of par-ticipation that are structured to open the practice to non-members.[34]

With respect to the processes of learning about Christ, being edu-cated into Christ, and participating in Christ, this is most helpful.

It may be thought, though, that it is with respect to the church

[32] Though see also the sixth observation below, where the significance of a group's subject matter is taken up.
[33] J. Lave and E. Wenger, *Situated Learning: Legitimate Peripheral Participation*, Cambridge: Cambridge University Press, 1991. The concept of 'community of practice' is developed especially in Chapter 4. LPP is in turn picked up in E. Wenger, *Communities of Practice: Learning, Meaning, and Identity*, Cambridge, Cambridge University Press, 1998, pp. 100–1.
[34] Wenger, *Communities of Practice*, p. 100.

– as the only community which explicitly practises the presence of Christ – that these insights are most pertinent. Certainly they do apply to the church, and I shall return to their relevance in Chapter 6. However, I want to argue strongly, fifth, that restricting the pertinence of LPP to the church alone is profoundly mistaken. Such an argument is, after all, in keeping with my resistance to ecclesiocentrism in Christian thought and practice (on Christocentric grounds) and builds upon the evidence provided in both this chapter and in the first two sections of the next. People are practising the presence of Christ by increasingly participating in Christ as they are being formed as persons in *a whole range of communities of practice* in which they are involved. Unless this practice of belonging to multiple communities of practice is respected there will be little chance to articulate an appropriately worldly (lay) spirituality based on people's actual experiences as they engage in many communities in their attempt to be human. And if we fail to understand and express this adequately, then our religiosity will have got the better of us. Rather than inform and transform daily living, we will have continued to separate sacred from secular and leave much of everyday life untouched by the benefits of theological interpretation.[35]

Sixth, *subject matter is important*. River engineers and those studying waste-disposal mechanisms can legitimately argue not only for the theological significance of their work (stewardship of the earth) but also for its vital importance in creating healthy human societies within which communities of practice can form. Manufacturers of curtain rings might have less of a case. But it would be wrong to claim that all educational groups, whatever their topics of study, are inevitably of equal relevance to the task of grasping what it means for Christ to take social form as a community of practice. The 'intangible outcomes' of a community of practice remain, regardless of the topic of study.

---

[35] This fifth observation does not, of course, only pertain to educational groups. My point here is that respect for the multiple communities of practice to which we all belong as human beings takes us beyond 'church' and that the way in which educational groups function can prove especially helpful for our perception of what is occurring in all of the communities of practice in which we participate.

But yet more may emerge in groups which have as their focus the study of, say, human society, psychology or education itself.[36]

Seventh, a significant difference between the worlds of work and education is that the latter pays much closer attention directly to *the life-stage* at which one is studying. It is no longer true that the path from school into higher education is straightforward (and likely for only a few). The move towards mass higher education in the UK reflects a similar trend throughout the developed world and means that many more participate in university courses than was the case two decades ago. But such participation happens in a greater variety of ways (many more part-time and distance-learning options) and at different stages of life. Many students are 'mature' (over 21) and may even be retired. Furthermore, schools have become 'community colleges' and find a mixture of children, young people and adults on their premises throughout the day and into the evenings. The contexts within which learning groups form are therefore more diverse.

Re-entry to formal education in later life does, of course, present huge challenges for both student and tutor. As an educator, I have experienced stark forms of regression on the part of students for whom 'education' means 'school' and school may, in the past, have been an unhappy experience. Even though a student might have been keen to undertake a particular module, the rekindling of unpleasant memories of any kind of 'classroom' can have detrimental effects on his or her behaviour and capacity to learn. When this kind of regression occurs, highly capable professional

---

[36] This is, of course, why in the entry requirements for those coming into theological education exemptions can be given for past study of some subjects and not others. Sometimes there can be exemptions for 'graduates of any discipline'; at other times more specific study needs to be proven. Also pertinent to this discussion: I see no reason for alarm that theology as a discipline is often located within Schools of Humanities, as opposed to remaining detached as a School or Faculty of Divinity or Theology. The interplay between theology and literary studies, history, philosophy and religious studies remains important. The greater challenge, perhaps, is to ensure that its inter-disciplinary risk-taking extends into Social and Life Sciences – psychology, sociology and cultural and media studies.

people sometimes seem unable to transfer the skills from their main job of work to the learning environment.[37]

None of this should be seen as counter-evidence, however, to the possibility that educational groups can be communities of practice in which Christ takes shape in social form. On the contrary: the evidence is even stronger that educational groups can be life-changing in so far as they provide contexts in which people can experience, in a safe environment, substantial personal growth. People thus take up courses at a great many different life-stages. But sensitive tutoring means that whatever is studied is undertaken in relation to the life-stage at which a person enters. It is a significantly different matter, for example, for a person who begins to study a language in her 50s, compared to beginning aged 11. But the cultural, and personal-developmental aspects of language-learning may prove more life-transforming, or just as life-transforming though in a different way.

A few years back I was theological consultant to the annual conference of further education (FE) chaplains in the UK. The life-changing role of education was very evident in the stories exchanged and reflected upon in the context of that conference. The further education sector in particular is a part of the education system in the UK that gives people a 'second chance'. It is very often participated in by people who, for whatever reason, did not take advantage of educational opportunities available to them first time round. In the educational communities of practice in which they then participate as learners, the degree of personal development they experience and the extent to which they discover an identity provide evidence that they are being formed as people. Christ is present in that process of person-formation.

An eighth observation relates both to work and education settings, and yet builds especially on the previous point, and is more likely to be developed explicitly in an educational context. I am referring to *the holistic aspect of education*. This coheres well with a sense of the presence of Christ in social form, for it is as whole

---

[37] And part of what they can then learn through their participation in a module (be it about systematic theology, biblical study or church history) is why they have reacted in this way: a further 'intangible outcome' which may prove to be the best kind of learning! The relevance of this insight to 'church' as a social form and to the church's participation in education should be noted here.

persons that we relate to others and thus as whole persons that we are 'in Christ'.

'Holistic spirituality' has been a fashionable term in recent years. The holistic approach 'is inclusive and takes seriously the knowledge-bearing capacity not only of the mind, but also of the body, emotions, senses, imagination, feelings, intuition and dreams'.[38] More attention will be given to the relationship of mind and body in Chapter 7 when I make use of recent work on situated cognition and recent thinking about the mind. For the moment it is worth noting that it is in educational contexts where attention to the whole person often first takes shape. It is itself an aspect of the spirituality of education, even if the term 'spirituality' may not always be used.

A holistic approach to education and theology may be easy to talk about, though difficult to carry out in practice, of course. Such an approach is necessary, however, if we are to do justice to what happens to us as people. Education and theology have far too easily become solely cerebral activities. However, as highly influential education theorist Jerome Bruner says: 'Why should an interest in cognition preclude feelings and emotions? Surely emotions and feelings are represented in the processes of meaning making and in our constructions of reality.'[39] Attention to the social form of Christ in educational contexts thus respects that participation in Christ is a whole-person experience. And such an educational insight links with theology's need to do more than perpetuate a tradition *about* Christ, at cost to giving attention to an experience *of* Christ.

Not only is participation a whole-person experience, it is also, finally, *a lifelong process*. There is currently widespread social concern for education as a lifelong phenomenon.[40] 'Lifelong learning' may be a political programme and a government catchword. But its relevance to spiritual development, and to participation in social forms of human existence in which Christ takes shape,

[38] W. Au, 'Holistic Spirituality', *New Dictionary of Christian Spirituality*, p. 342.
[39] J. Bruner, *The Culture of Education*, Cambridge, Mass. and London: Harvard University Press, 1996, p. 12.
[40] 'Spiritual formation . . . must remain continuous, since the Christian remains in a position of discipleship for the whole of life. The secular concept of lifelong learning echoes this understanding', G. Simmonds, 'Formation, Spiritual', *New Dictionary of Christian Spirituality*, p. 310.

deserves close attention. It is a counter to a view that one has met Christ in a conversion experience in the past and then lived off the riches of that experience, or to the idea that one meets Christ in church, or in the context of formal worship alone. Paying life-long, holistic attention to who and where Christ is present involves looking always at a great variety of social contexts in which person-formation occurs.

And what of Christ in all of this?

If we now 'work back' from the social forms in which we see Christ present to what we can actually say about Christ, where does this take us?

Christ as a 'person'

The first insight we gain is that *Christ is a person*. This is more significant than it may seem at first. Christ is a person rather than 'personhood personified'. Calling Christ a person stresses the embodied nature of Christ, as opposed to some ideal notion which awaits enfleshment. Christ is a person, not an individual. The way in which God acts in the world in continuity with the life, death and resurrection of Jesus occurs in the form of a 'corporate person'. As we now know, a person is not simply an individual. A person comprises an individual body and a whole set of relationships. A person's identity/identities result from that person's interactions with others.

In the same way that Jesus of Nazareth needs to be seen in the context of the movement that he initiated, so also the continuing presence of the person of Christ is comprehensible only in the context of interaction between embodied beings. Those who are 'in Christ' – whether aware of it or not – are formed as persons through personal interaction. Christ finds form as a social body in which people participate through the patterns of relating described in Chapter 2.

Reaffirming the personal nature of Christ in this way forces us to rethink the glib way in which we might use the phrase 'the person of Christ'. For much of Christian tradition, dogmatics and systematic theology have spoken of the 'person and work of

Christ'. Up until the modern period, and the rise of the 'Quest of the Historical Jesus', this would clearly have gone beyond the life and death of Jesus of Nazareth. Interpreting the resurrection meant giving attention to the continuing impact and presence of God as God worked through the Spirit, which was also Christ's Spirit. The historical Quest challenged the equating – relatively easy until then – of Jesus, Christ and Spirit. Suddenly, the 'person and work of Christ' could be more easily left in the past. Furthermore, the continuing sense of the presence of the Christ in the church (as Christ's body), which the age of Christendom had been able to maintain, was then open to challenge from many directions. The church was not all that it was cracked up to be (and orthodoxy might be deceptive), and human culture always was, or was becoming, much more complicated than the easy equation of Jesus, Christ and Spirit, and the cultural dominance of the church, allowed for.

The Quest has now made its point. Jesus of Nazareth, the historical figure, is far from irrelevant for Christology, but does not determine everything that Christology can and must do. Christendom has gone, but the churches still exist as social structures and have work to do in complex societies where pluralism is the reality. In this context, the reaffirmation that Christ is a (collective) person becomes even more important than has been the case throughout much of Christian history. It is my contention that exploring Christ with reference to the concept of 'community of practice' enables us to pay the necessary attention to Christ as corporate person, in a way that is fruitful for how human life is now lived.

The hidden Christ

A second insight from our exploration of Christ as a community of practice is that Christ may be present despite the basic intentions of a group. In fact, any group that works as a community of practice is in the business of person-forming and, from a Christian perspective, such a group participates in Christ. Nonetheless, Christ may be *a hidden presence*. This being so, to identify the presence of Christ simply or largely as 'church' is both theologically misleading and socially damaging. Recognizing that Christ takes multiple social forms in the world demands that a creative and imaginative approach be adopted to the task of identifying who, what and where Christ is today.

Similarly it seems unwise to use the notion of 'anonymous Christians'. This concept was important in its own time as a challenge to the church's ecclesiocentrism. The danger of the term is that it merely replaces ecclesiocentrism with an effortless claim of superiority by Christianity. By contrast, the concept of the hidden Christ keeps Christians in their appropriate (limited) place. Christians have a task to attempt to grasp what God in Christ is doing in the world. This is what Christology is for. But a concept of the hidden Christ retains a sense for Christians too that they have yet more about Christ to discover.

Two words of caution still have to be sounded, though. First, the definition of Christ may be in danger of becoming too predetermined. Exploring Christ in terms of community of practice may lead us to look at neat, already-existing, self-contained communities as the place where God is most active. But what about the margins? What about the people who don't fit, who don't think of themselves as loved and included, or politically empowered? Communities of practice can, of course, be political and can unite otherwise marginal people. But it would be wrong to claim that a community of practice enables all to be said about Christ that needs to be said. Christ challenges all attempts to grasp or encapsulate Christ. This must be a fundamental tenet of Christology.

Second, Christ must not become a mere symbol for 'personal development'. Christology entails personal development. In Christian perspective, personal development is enhanced by being interpreted christologically. But all that is labelled 'personal development' is not necessarily Christology. Person-forming happens anywhere, and is of significance for Christology, but 'Christ' is not simply the sum total of all examples of person-formation. Recognition of a wide range of settings in which person-formation occurs, and thus where Christ in social form struggles to take shape, challenges narrow Christologies and theologies. But Christ is not subsumed within other discourses about the human self. Rather, broad exploration of the person of Christ in the terms described in this book contributes to a fuller investigation of what it means to be human than much contemporary public discussion permits. Theology thus reclaims its rightful place at the round table at which psychologists, sociologists, philosophers, artists of all kinds, anthropologists and cultural theorists now sit.

A critical postscript

My children are doubtful that there can be any possibility of life in secondary education (high school) being a context for glimpses of the reign of God. And the thought that school classes, or learning groups, may function as communities of practice, and be social forms in which Christ can be seen to be present, is met with even greater scepticism. But our conversation is a lively one and has included the following considerations.

First, the contemporary classroom is in many cases a microcosm of multifaith Western societies. If God in Christ is to be evident in the world today, then this will necessarily occur in some complex contexts of interfaith encounter. This being so, a multifaith classroom may prove a fine example of where Christ becomes evident. For it is here, in the midst of interfaith encounter, where person-formation is occurring. This is, of course, a Christian reading of what is going on. But if Christ is present in a multifaith classroom, then the Christian church is being challenged in its own readings of who and where Christ is in the world today. 'You are the body of Christ' takes on a slightly different meaning from Paul. But it may be an appropriate Christian interpretation, in continuity with Paul, of what is happening, or can happen, in schools.

Second, school education is a prime time of personal growth and identity formation. It is an early stage in a lifelong process. Whatever names are given to, and whatever interpretations are offered of, this process, its importance cannot be overestimated. Personal growth and identity formation are aspects of spiritual development, despite the debates that may rage about whether religious education does or should contribute to the understanding of how personal growth occurs. In terms of the discussion conducted in this chapter, however, it is important to note that person-formation and holistic growth belong together. Both of these belong, in Christian understanding, 'in Christ'. Where they are occurring, then Christ is present. If they occur in school, then Christ is clearly there.

Third, school is a crucial social group through which identity formation happens beyond the family, perhaps especially for those who do not have a religious community to relate to, or do not relate easily to a religious or any other formative community in early life.

In oscillating, then, between family and school, two unchosen social contexts,[41] young people begin to make their first choices about friendships and lifestyles. Who they associate with, and are therefore co-formed by, become crucial in identity formation and therefore in the extent to which they participate in being formed in Christ.[42]

These topics, all of them worthy of longer discussion, illustrate clearly how essential it is to reflect on person-formation and what social form Christ takes in relation to everyday life. In her helpful article on 'Adolescents and Spirituality' in *The New SCM Dictionary of Christian Spirituality*, Rebecca Nye comments:

> A primary spiritual need for adolescent faith is to develop identity through relationship . . . Youth spirituality may be best served in terms of Christ-like relating – through accepting and accompanying, rather than dictating the criteria of belief and behaviour on adult terms.[43]

This is surely accurate. It does, though, indicate that, in the context of school education, friendships as communities of practice are themselves forms of the presence of Christ, and that the emergence of a wider network of support for such friendships contributes to the development of a spirituality.

---

[41] In the UK, though 'choice' is a crucial feature of current debates about school education, in practice the term is misused. Parents state preferences within a limited range of options. It is therefore accurate – certainly from a pupil's point of view – to speak of school as an unchosen social context.

[42] I stress here that this is not simply an issue about 'churchgoing'. Church is essential for an active, conscious process of being formed 'in Christ'. But because Christ is not bound to or by that which constituted 'church', then being formed in Christ is inevitably not bound to churchgoing as a social practice.

[43] R. Nye, 'Adolescents and Spirituality', *New Dictionary of Christian Spirituality*, p. 86.

In this critical postscript, reflecting out of my own domestic life on the limitations and possibilities of one form of education as a location in which Christ may be present in social form, I have mentioned family, friends and church. An ideal bridge has therefore been constructed to the next chapter.

6 Christ as community of practice (III): Family, friends and church

Having introduced the concept of 'community of practice' in Chapter 4, I devoted Chapter 5 to the exposition of two possible contexts in which Christ may take social form as a community of practice. It may have seemed surprising that I did not begin either with church, or with what may be regarded as more fundamental forms of human life, above all the family. I was, however, seeking to relate to the world out of which the concept of 'community of practice' emerged (work and education). I was also acknowledging by such a procedure that I was still operating within the conceptual terrain mapped out by Bonhoeffer. 'Labour' was one of the mandates he identified as meriting exploration within the task of identifying the forms in which Christ is present in the world.

Two of Bonhoeffer's other mandates remain to be explored in some form: marriage and church.[1] Arguably these are, in Christian understanding, more basic forms of human community. In the forms in which I shall examine them – family/household and church – they represent a form of social unit which no human being has chosen and none can avoid (family) and the quintessential explicit and conscious form in which Christians lay claim to be participating in Christ's body (church). Between these two forms of social living, I shall also explore a third form: friendship. Friendship features among Bonhoeffer's 'spheres of freedom' rather than the 'mandates'. As his life and work indicate, however, this was as important a theological category as the four mandates he listed.

[1] Bonhoeffer's fourth 'mandate' – government – was considered in Chapter 3.

Christ in the family

Experience of family life, whether good or bad, is formative.[2] If, therefore, Christ takes social form, then the role of family – positive and negative – in the task of discovering who and where Christ is in the world today is a vital area of enquiry. If, furthermore, Christ takes social form in the family as community of practice, then the family needs very careful scrutiny indeed. There is much lazy theology about the family in Christianity. Many easy (ultimately idolatrous) appeals are made to the family's sanctity and there are many unspoken assumptions at work about the family through the church.[3] I begin from the premise that a positive, life-enhancing understanding of 'family life' in some form needs to be found for the sake of society's well-being. But it cannot be anticipated at the outset what that form might be.

Rita Nakashima Brock, whose work was considered in Chapter 6 of *Christ in Focus*, sets the agenda. In drawing attention to the need for a christological critique of the patriarchal family, Brock has shown how models of family can negatively control the reception and exploration of images of Christ. Her work urges that Christologies be worked out that are not constrained by bad relationships. In this way they can seek to avoid being destructive. If Christ is to be identified at work in family life, and to be spoken of on the basis of family experience, then we must do this with a realism about family life while also offering a potentially transformative account of what families can achieve.

We are faced with a major difficulty. If God in Christ becomes evident as, and in, relationships, then who and what God in Christ is must somehow be identifiable. However, if the primary

---

[2] I have drawn here on sociological, and social psychological as well as theological literature, including: K. Barth, *Church Dogmatics III/4*, Edinburgh: T & T Clark, 1961; W. Green, *The Future of the Family*, London: Mowbray, 1984; S. Duck, *Relating to Others* (2nd edn), Buckingham and Philadelphia: Open University Press, 1999; R. Clapp, *Families at the Crossroads*, Downers Grove: InterVarsity Press, 1993; A. Borrowdale, *Reconstructing Family Values*, London: SPCK, 1994; S. C. Barton (ed.), *The Family in Theological Perspective*, Edinburgh: T & T Clark, 1996; D. Browning et al., *From Culture Wars to Common Ground: Religion and the American Family Debate*, Louisville: Westminster John Knox Press, 1997; and H. Wilkinson (ed.), *Family Business*, London: Demos, 2000.

[3] The explorations by Clapp and by Loughlin in Barton (ed.), *The Family* are especially helpful here.

relationships through which we are forged as people profoundly affect how we can conceive of God in Christ, then Christ may be hard to make out. Dysfunctional formative human groups may actually prove obstacles to the possibility of Christ taking social form in the world.[4]

We could, of course, seek to make an appeal to revelation in a way that would bypass the dilemma. Following Karl Barth, we could, for example, stress that God alone is a Father.[5] Therefore, because all fatherhood derives from God, it could be claimed that there is no real sense in which we can work back from the human experience of parenting and family life to any conclusions about who and where God in Christ is. I do not take this route because theological exploration is more messy than such neatness permits.[6] As argued in Chapter 2 of *Christ in Focus*, there is a constant dialogue going on in theology between tradition and experience, and people start at different places and have different focal points. Here I am starting from experience, recognizing that I am still 'traditioned' as I do so. This means that I think I know something of what I am looking for when I try to locate Christ within family life. At the same time, I am expecting to be challenged by the Christ I find (otherwise I am claiming to have theology 'sorted' before I even start). Though I can therefore still speak quite happily of the *revelation* of God in Christ, I wish to do so only on the basis of having found a way through the complexity of human inter-relationship, rather than trying to avoid it.

Families and households

How, then, does Christ take social form in family life? First, 'family' must be defined. Anne Borrowdale refers to three understandings: kith and kin, the household and the nuclear family.[7] The 'household' is essentially a sociological term, pertaining to

[4] Jeff Astley refers to 'the *miseducative* dynamics' (his italics) which can occur in family life ('The Role of the Family in the Formation and Criticism of Faith' in Barton (ed.), *The Family*, p. 199).
[5] K. Barth, *Church Dogmatics* III/4, p. 245.
[6] Barth knew this, of course, but his emphasis on the priority of revelation was so conceptually important to him that his work sometimes seems not to allow for the fact that he knew about theological messiness.
[7] Borrowdale, *Reconstructing*, ch. 3.

the basic group out of which a person operates. It is likely, though not inevitable, that whatever social pattern surrounds this base, some key relationships will be at work within the 'household'. As patterns of social living evolve, however, it is becoming clear that the notion of 'household' is taking on a fresh significance.[8] As people settle later into child-rearing partnerships and either live alone, or choose to form households with friends, then the formative family-like structure of the household becomes increasingly more important.[9] 'Kinship' refers to family groupings based on extended relations (many generations, including aunts, uncles and cousins), while 'nuclear families' are two-generational, comprising one or two parents and immediate offspring.

The distinction between kinship and the nuclear family often accentuates cultural differences. African-Caribbean, Asian and white English working-class people, for example, often relate to a wide network of family relations (extended family) as opposed to an immediate, nuclear family. These patterns are changing gradually, with some evidence of resistance, for example, among younger African-Caribbean parents to the demands of strong, clear kinship ties. Generally, it remains the case that much rhetoric – political, Christian and common – about 'the family' usually has the nuclear family firmly in mind. However, it is not necessarily in the nuclear family that people experience the formative relationships with respect to which contemporary exploration of Christ might best occur.

This first, descriptive, point invites us to reflect on where we have enjoyed our primary and most significant early experiences of human relationship. Examining 'family' means exploring the social form of a primary unit, a 'basic community', in and through which a person's identity first emerges and is shaped.

---

[8] See, for example, the work of David Matkzo McCarthy, *Sex and Love in the Home*, London: SCM Press, 2001, the subtitle of which is 'A Theology of the Household'. McCarthy does, however, appear to conceive of 'household' rather more closely only to groupings of blood relations than I do here.

[9] E. Moltmann-Wendell is, it seems to me, quite correct in her observation that: 'a cultural change is taking place in which family ties and family norms are fading into the background and being replaced by the most diverse kinds of groups of friends, on the same footing as the family or as a substitute for it' (*Rediscovering Friendship*, London: SCM Press, 2000, p. 3). There is therefore an overlap and a mutually critical correlation between this section of the chapter and the next ('Christ among friends').

Most readers are likely to have experienced such community in the company of blood relations. However, whether or not this is the case, whether or not we choose to continue to live in some pattern of family/household life with blood relations, and whether or not we have children ourselves, there is no escaping the formative nature of some form of 'family'. In using the term 'basic community' I am offering an allusion to the base communities identified in liberation theology, formative communities in which one's self is developed through prayerful exploration of faith, community and politics. In current Western use, however, such communities are usually assumed to be chosen in adult life. By 'basic community' I am trying to find a term that accentuates the formative nature of 'the family', in both early and later life, recognizing that we are formed by other groups – very often groups of blood relations, or relationships formed by marriage or marriage-like partnerships – which we do not choose. Furthermore, our 'family' remains our family into adulthood, and we may continue to choose to live with people (parents, siblings) whom we have not chosen.

It is also important to note a tension shown in the language used, between 'emerging' identities and identities being 'shaped' (or even 'constructed'). I cannot enter into extensive discussion on this matter here. I wish simply to note that there are at least two ways in which a person's identity takes form. There are aspects of the self which are clearly constrained by biology, chemistry and environment. Yet these influences need not be viewed as wholly deterministic of the self. The self does not appear to be the result solely of the activity of genes or the influence of surroundings. The self is shaped by something further than these influences over which one has little control, even if a post-Enlightenment view of a wholly autonomous self may prove wide of the mark.[10]

In talking of the family as a basic community, then, I am urging that attention be paid to whatever formative communities we have grown up in (whether blood families or not), through which we have undertaken our first lessons in human relationships. It is from these formative experiences, and in the light of the critiques

---

[10] Hence, I resist referring to the 'construction of the self' in any unqualified way. This seems to me to claim too much.

we offer of them, that we come to understand what we deem good and bad relationships to be. Christologically speaking, it can only be with regard to such experiences – good or bad – that we can begin to discern what a relationship 'with' or 'in' Christ might be.

'Family' as a community of practice

Having identified what our primary social unit might have been, we must begin to examine more fully what it is that this social form of living achieves, and why it may therefore be considered as a form of Christ, as a community of practice. What is it that family life 'practises'?

Two points came to the fore in Chapter 5's discussion of communities of practice in work and education contexts. These were the role of communities of practice in the formation of persons and the fact that such formation often occurs as an 'intangible outcome', alongside the primary task of the community. With a family it is significantly different. Families exist for the purpose of forming persons. Families – in the broadest sense in which I am using the term – are the primary contexts in which love, justice and power can be discovered and explored. For all people, some form of family (kinship, household or nuclear group) will have provided a social space within which love/hate, justice/injustice and power/powerlessness have first been wrestled with, however much their early discoveries may have been examined and re-examined, reworked, owned or disowned. As Astley rightly notes, the family 'is the place where the self learns not to be selfish: where it learns the attitudes, dispositions and skills of sharing, responsibility and altruism at a deep, because unreflective, level'.[11] Even more pithily, but still with a respect for the safety and importance of family life at its best, 'families are places you go to, to have your arguments'.[12] If, then, Christocentrism is ultimately about the centrality of the formation of human persons 'in Christ', then any formative groups become christologically significant. Exploration of the presence of

---

[11] Astley, 'The Role of the Family', p. 194.
[12] I have not been able to trace the source of this quotation, but remain grateful to whoever said it!

God in Christ must inevitably engage with understandings of family and family-like structures.

Third, the level of intimacy within families should be stressed. It is only in the intimacy of a family, or family-like group, that all of the potential for discovery and exploration just mentioned can be fulfilled. It is as a result of this intimacy, and through participation in some of the human relationships existing within families, that Christian theologians have found some of the basic categories with which to work: God as Father, Jesus as brother, for example. Instantly, though, the limitations are also apparent: why not mother or sister? And why use only male labels for God? Why allow the maleness of Jesus to control the family categories used of God? What does the maleness of Jesus do to the emerging possibilities of 'relationship with Jesus', respectively, for boys and girls, young men and young women, as they seek to explore faith, prayer, spirituality and theology? The limitations of blood family imagery for describing all that needs to be said about God, and about God's relationships to humankind, thus become apparent.

What families achieve

So, we all have family-like groups which we need critically to reflect upon; these groups are intended to be person-forming; and the level of intimacy present within them and the language used to express it have been deeply influential theologically. But we must move beyond these observations and examine what and how families and family-like structures contribute to the formation of persons. How do they enable the wrestling with love/hate, justice/injustice and power/powerlessness to occur? And how and why can they be regarded as forms of Christ as a result?

A number of features of family life are crucial in this respect. *Mutuality* is at the heart of what a family offers at its best. Each member gives and receives from others with equal regard.[13] In a family, this equal regard can be felt, even without all members of the group being equal in every way. Differences between generations create dynamics and power relations in families, which

[13] Browning et al., *From Culture Wars*, ch. 10.

produce hierarchies. These are not simple hierarchies. Sometimes they harden to the extent that they stifle attempts to bring about mutuality. In such a case, the necessary family roles do not adapt to create space for mutual regard. But at their best, families do offer this mutual regard, despite the unevenness (even inequality) that different roles produce.[14] Where appropriate differentiation happens, then the family does not divide into hierarchies which prevent growth of parents and children alike.

Emotional security is a second component which families can provide. Without such security, a person (and not merely when a young child) is less able to feel confident in their own identity and in relating to others in a wide variety of social situations. It is the consistent checking back with one's 'emotional base' that enables a person to 'be' in relation to others. People do not cease to need such an emotional base in later life. It is merely the form of the base that may change: a new family pattern, a family-like set of relationships in a new household or set of friendships.

Third, families play a crucial role in enabling people to learn 'the delicate balancing act of *being separate together*'.[15] What the psychologists call 'individuation' occurs appropriately in families when a child learns what it means to be an individual in her own right. That this process occurs in a setting where there is still the complexity of being with others highlights the fact that individuation does not result in carefree autonomy, but 'must be balanced by interdependence'.[16] The interplay between independence and interdependence is directly pertinent to what it means to be in Christ, given that the individual has the opportunity to encounter God in Christ, yet is also always dependent on others in order to be in Christ. Christ is present not simply as the sum total of individual experiences, but in a social form in which individuals participate.

If families are places where people go to have their arguments, then they are places where conflict happens. As Anne Borrowdale rightly remarks, 'We must avoid acting out of a belief that conflict is sinful, that in an ideal family, people do not argue.'[17] As

---

[14] McCarthy, *Sex and Love in the Home*, p. 188.

[15] Astley, 'The Role of the Family', p. 194 (my emphasis).

[16] Astley, 'The Role of the Family', p. 194.

[17] A. Borrowdale, 'Right Relations: Forgiveness and Family Life' in Barton (ed.), *The Family*, pp. 203–17, here p. 205.

locations where conflict happens, families are therefore places where people begin to grapple with what it means to forgive and be forgiven.[18] Learning 'to say sorry' (and actually mean it) or finally to say 'it's OK' (rather than 'it doesn't matter') after a family altercation lie at the heart of the way that a family models and embodies the grace which needs the enfleshment of social life if we are to grasp it as human beings. In christological perspective, when someone forgives, they are not simply imitating Christ as if this were an individual's moral decision to choose to act in this way. Forgiving and being forgiven are forms of participation in the presence of God in Christ in the world today. People who forgive and are forgiven are held within God when forgiveness occurs. They participate in a gracious, divine act which goes beyond what the individuals do, for love from God, of a depth too deep for words, enables them to do what they might otherwise not do.

Hospitality is also a hallmark of family life at its best. From an emotionally secure base, however meagre their material means might be, families can befriend and support others. Clapp offers an intriguing slant on the theme of hospitality in noting the way in which children are themselves strangers to their parents, who welcome them into the world by welcoming them into a family. Children in turn educate their parents who 'learn a little about being out of control, about the possibility of surprise (and so of hope), about how strange we [i.e. those who are parents] ourselves are'.[19]

Welcoming strangers – those who are not blood relations – can also be learned in the context of a family. In this way, insight is gained both into what the family has achieved (a security and stability on the basis of which others can be welcomed in) and what it can model of human community beyond itself: that is, a hospitable family can open its members' eyes to the possibility of a hospitable society. The practice of hospitality is thus profoundly christological in that it reflects a person's security of identity in Christ, and embodies Christ's welcoming of the stranger.

Finally, as places of conflict, forgiveness and hospitality, families are *political life in microcosm*.[20] As Susan Parsons recognizes,

[18] Astley, 'The Role of the Family', p. 196.
[19] Clapp, *Families*, p. 148.
[20] McCarthy, *Sex and Love in the Home*, pp. 140–1.

the family must be seen as 'a school of justice, and the just family the essential foundation for a just society'.[21] Power relations, and critical scrutiny of the way that power is wielded, begin in the context of family life. Economic power is a crucial and frequently overlooked aspect of family life: the question of who controls the distribution of whatever income a family receives. Handling the tensions of decision-making in the context of a family's person-forming task is, of course, a colossal task. Yet it is here, in the context of the family, that perhaps Christology's sharpest challenge is faced. All manifestations of the intensity and complexity of human relations can be discerned here. If Christ cannot be discerned here, or if the presence of God in Christ cannot break through here, then fully human relations – relations understood by Christians to be 'in Christ' – may be possible nowhere. For this reason, it becomes appropriate to speak also of a 'politics of Christology'. Attempting to discern and to speak of Christ today requires the speaker to address how people relate in society.

These six features of family living – mutuality, emotional security, being separate together, forgiving and being forgiven, hospitality and politics – are expressions of love as love takes shape in human life. They turn a core term of theology, and a reality which non-theists also acknowledge as worth working with (love), into the detail and complexity of actual living. They link with the christological framework provided in Chapter 2. It is in the midst of a family's struggle to be shaped by these six features that it is possible for echoes of the story of Jesus to shape contemporary living. The narratives about Jesus become more than stories about someone else. They invite readers and hearers to perform and embody a particular form of human living.

The family is thus a third social form in which Christ is present, a third form of Christ as a community of practice. It is quite different from the contexts of work and education. It could be argued to be more crucial than either of those, for it is unavoidable. However, I would not want to make any simple judgement about the relative importance of the social forms being considered. Christ can take all of the five forms, and may take all five forms for some people. It cannot be predicted which will prove

[21] S. Parsons, 'Feminism and the Family' in Barton (ed.), *The Family*, p. 275.

most determinative for those who seek to live, or discover what it means to be, 'in Christ' as a human being.

However, without identifying such concrete social forms as manifestations of the presence of Christ, the features identified in Chapter 2 have little chance of coming to fruition. God is incarnate in Christ, and for incarnation to be meaningful we have to be able to show where, among whom and in what form Christ is present.

Still, it may be argued that the features of human living identified here with respect to families are not experienced in families alone. Indeed, as acknowledged earlier, for some people they may not be experienced in families at all. This observation is important in two respects. First, it recognizes that the features of family life I have identified also occur in other forms of social living, friendships above all, as well as the form of life known as 'church'. At a time when Western culture is re-examining its primary social units, and when forms of religious life often do not feature on the map, the interplay of family/kinship/household structures, friendship and church/religious social life will become increasingly important. In christological perspective, the search for a fully human life, life in Christ, will inevitably draw on this critical interplay.

Second, recognition that this critical interplay happens *at all* is an important corrective to the tendency in some forms of Christianity to idolize either the family or the church. If, as recognized in *Christ in Focus*, there is a danger of Christianity erring towards ecclesiocentrism when it considers how human life is best structured, then one counter to that tendency has taken the form of overemphasis upon the family.[22] Families do not always achieve what they set out to achieve. They are not always good

[22] Clapp notes this and wants to put church before family. While I agree with his attempt to challenge the idolization of the family, I am not clear that his own remedy does not veer off in the wrong direction. Clapp is right to say that 'we cannot put Jesus first and still put family first' (Clapp, *Families*, p. 68), but may be wrong in his claim that 'Restoring and redeeming the family . . . does not begin with the nation or with the family itself. It begins with the church' (*Families*, p. 47). I prefer to say that church is part of the solution as one of the social forms of Christ which critiques, and is critiqued by, experience of being 'family', and other forms of social living. It is the experience of diverse forms of social living, and the mutual critique between them, in theological perspective, which enables us to get a better grasp of what it means to participate in Christ.

things. They do not always enable the full development of persons. They often damage people deeply and carry within them considerable pain. As those who conduct funerals testify, there is very often much unresolved hurt within families which is exposed at the time of a death. It would therefore be ill advised to suggest that families are somehow inevitably the main social context in which Christ is to be discerned and participated in.[23]

As a formative group in the development of human relationships, then, the family proves no less decisive for theology and Christology than it does in sociology and psychology. But family models of relationships will not of themselves suffice for christological exploration. Experience of other forms of human relationship are needed to enable comparison with, critical reflection upon and, as necessary, correction of early family experiences to be made. These comparisons are part of the process of theological reflection as understandings of Christ evolve.[24]

An easy conclusion to draw would be that family experiences are somehow left behind in this process. They need not be, of course. Family rhetoric remains theologically useful, even if it is limited. God may remain father and Christ may remain brother, for those for whom these terms remain vibrant and positive. But as we saw above, it is worth asking whether many forms of the image of the fatherhood of God have helped Christian believers to grow up. Some remain with an infantile faith. Similarly, Christ may also remain as always the rather avuncular 'older brother' who leads, protects and yet may also prevent full growth. We need more than experiences of family, and more than images of God and Christ drawn from family life, to do justice to the experience of participation in Christ. It is therefore to the theme of friendship that we now turn.

---

[23] It is for this reason that I have resisted developing the notion of the family (in whatever form) as 'domestic church'. Though this term is helpful in so far as it recognizes a family's role in the spiritual formation of all its members, it allies the form of family life too closely with that of structured Christianity. In so doing it becomes another form of ecclesiocentrism which leaves insufficient scope for Christ to take form in many and diverse ways in human social living.

[24] R. N. Brock, *Journeys by Heart: A Christology of Erotic Power*, New York: Crossroad, 1988, pp. 3–4, 23, 103.

Christ among friends

It is staggering how little theological reflection can be found on the concept of friendship within the Christian tradition.[25] Yet, if we are to learn who Christ is by examining actual experiences of human relationship, then human friendships are a really important example to explore. Christ is not present only in families, working and educational settings, nor even only in the form of church. Even if family members and other Christians are friends to us, the nature of that friendship is worthy of separate examination. It is all the more crucial to explore how friendships beyond the identifiable church, and outside of families, become locations of Christ's presence. Exploration of Christ 'among friends' will likely help us better understand pastoral aspects of Christianity – faith development and human growth – and lead in turn to a more expansive Christology than we often work with in the church.

Defining friendship today

It is worth recording how, in contemporary Western culture, the 'friend' has developed as a primary relationship over and above the family. A recent British TV game show has moved beyond the normal family teams to teams of friends, for example. It is now assumed that it is among peer-group friendships, rather than among families, that the deepest joys and disap-

---

[25] See, for example, J. Nelson, *The Intimate Connection,* London: SPCK, 1992, p. 47; Moltmann-Wendell, *Rediscovering,* p. 16. The most comprehensive survey of the limited resources available is E. H. (Liz) Carmichael, *Friendship: Interpreting Christian Love,* London: T&T Clark International, 2004. It is worth noting that sociologists, too, have not paid much attention either to friendship or to kinship (see e.g. Allan, *Kinship and Friendship,* p. 3). In what follows, in addition to Nelson, Moltmann-Wendell and Carmichael, I have used J. Moltmann, *The Church in the Power of the Spirit,* London: SCM Press, 1977: esp. III.6, G. Meilaender, *Friendship: A Study in Theological Ethics,* London and Notre Dame: University of Notre Dame Press, 1981, M. E. Hunt, *Fierce Tenderness: A Feminist Theology of Friendship,* New York: Crossroad, 1992, and E. Stuart, *Just Good Friends,* London: Mowbray, 1995. Beyond theology, in addition to Allan's work, I have used S. Duck, *Relating to Others,* Buckingham and Philadelphia: Open University Press, 1999.

pointments can be borne, the greatest risks taken and trusts expressed.[26]

A second example comes from the work of sociologist Graham Allan. Believing that kinship ties and social networks remain stronger than is often supposed, Allan does not fully support the privatization thesis that British citizens today have retreated from social interaction in their daily lives. However, he acknowledges that industrialization and urbanization have undoubtedly contributed to significant shifts in social patterns. Privatization and greater social mobility (in addition to other factors such as cohabitation and increased divorce rates) have complicated family patterns. Allan notes a gradual increase in the extent to which (in middle-class families, but also among the working class) the home has become the place where friendships are encouraged to develop (wherever they may begin). This suggests a significant evolution in social interaction, away from the inevitable primacy of family and towards the decisive importance of friendships in contemporary culture.[27]

So what, then, constitutes a friendship? What are we drawing on, in seeking to use friendships to inform Christology? I begin with three working definitions, one from a sociologist, two from theologians.[28] Graham Allan emphasizes quality, equality, reciprocity and solidarity. He writes:

> While there may occasionally be conflict between friends, the categorization of someone as a friend is based on the quality of the bond that there is . . . Friendship, in whatever form it takes, is defined as a relationship between equals. That is,

---

[26] This adds evidence to support Moltmann-Wendell's hunch, cited in n. 9 above. Such an idyllic picture of friendships will, of course, never have been wholly true of families in the past, or only true of families. But this cultural shift at least indicates a sharp change of perception and emphasis.

[27] Allan, *Kinship and Friendship*, pp. 87–8. I am not, of course, denying the crucial importance of family background; nor is Allan. Nor am I overlooking the fact that there are other issues involved here: that is, the 'privatization' of friendship may also present a contemporary problem. My point is simply to note the developing significance of friendship in contemporary society (or, as might be argued, its re-discovery, since the post-Reformation's overemphasis on marriage and family; see Stuart, *Just Good Friends*, p. 42).

[28] And all of these should be read in critical conversation with the six aspects of family life cited in the previous section. There is significant overlap in what families and friendships offer and achieve.

within friendship there is little sense of social hierarchy or status difference . . . Friendships in which there are marked inequalities or in which one side continually lays claim to social superiority over the other will not last long . . . [w]ith friendships, the need for reciprocity is an important principle . . . friendship is not about status hierarchy or difference; it is about solidarity on the basis of liking and trust.[29]

In addition, Allan points out that friendships are likely to be between people of similar ages. There is a material-exchange dimension – an informal economic to-and-fro arrangement – to the reciprocity involved. And, with the exception of friendships that become family relationships (through marriage/partnership and child-rearing), friendships tend mostly to be same-sex.[30]

All the hallmarks of friendship identified by Allan, and the further clarifications, suggest an interplay between friendship and 'being church' and also inform our understanding of Christ. For if the presence of Christ connects directly (and is in large part discovered through) particular friendships of a certain *kind* and *quality*, then it is important to identify the nature of those friendships.

A second definition of friendship comes from Jürgen Moltmann. For Moltmann, friendship includes reliance, affection, loyalty, promise and openness. Friendships provide the opportunity for the communication of joy. Only on this basis is the sharing of sorrow also possible. 'Friendship is the reasonable passion for truly human fellowship; it is a mutual affection cemented by loyalty. The more people begin to live with one another as friends, the more privileges and claims to domination become superfluous.'[31] For Moltmann, friendship lies beyond parent–child and master–slave relationships, and beyond relationships dependent upon one's sex. This point is crucial for the church to hear, both in its understanding and presentation of, and also in its modelling of, Christ in its own practice. For if, in Moltmann's terms, 'the friendship of Jesus' is to be discovered through the patterns of human friendship he describes, and churches are to be

---

[29] Allan, *Kinship and Friendship*, pp. 84, 89–90 and 97.
[30] Accepting that the picture is rendered more complicated by the existence of gay and lesbian partnerships and the fact that gay people sometimes seek to become parents and may in some contexts legally adopt children.
[31] Moltmann, *The Church*, p. 116.

societies of friends, then clarification of Christ through friendship can potentially exert a huge impact upon the church's self-perception and task.

Moltmann's 1977 book is about the church, not directly about Christ, and he develops his thesis through use of Ignatius of Antioch's well-known statement that 'wheresoever Christ Jesus is, there is the Catholic [i.e. universal] Church'.[32] An approach to Christology through friendship, however, raises questions about how the church in the present is to be understood.[33] For identifying where Christ is present does not lead directly to institutional forms of church. Moltmann's own answer to the question 'where, then, is Christ?' is threefold: in the apostolate, in the poor and in the parousia.[34] His first response values the institutional church, but in so far as it carries the apostolic witness and tradition within it. The second response is a major challenge to all churches, for Christ is here present, says Moltmann, 'in the latent brotherhood of the Judge hidden in the poor'.[35] Finally, Moltmann looks to the future, to 'the consummation of the history of liberation'.[36]

At this point, it would be fair to ask where the potentially radical insights gained through his Christology of friendship have actually taken him.[37] Admittedly, Moltmann has explored the limitation of friendship as a means of understanding the church. He has seen that it will take a major effort to shift privatized understandings of friendship more into the public realm.[38] This observation can prove useful to the approach to understanding Christ being developed here.[39] But all three aspects of his exploration of

---

[32] *'Ubi Christus – ibi ecclesia'* (Moltmann, *The Church*, pp. 122, 127 and 129); the relevant passage is cited in ET in, for example, H. Bettenson and C. Maunder, *Documents of the Christian Church*, Oxford : Oxford University Press, 1999, p. 69.

[33] See next section.

[34] Moltmann, *The Church*, pp. 123–32.

[35] Moltmann, *The Church*, p. 128.

[36] Moltmann, *The Church*, p. 132.

[37] See, for example, the statement: 'Through the friendship of Jesus the disciples become the free friends of God. In his fellowship they no longer experience God as Lord, and not merely as Father either; they experience him as a friend, in his innermost being' (Moltmann, *The Church*, p. 118).

[38] Moltmann, *The Church*, p. 121.

[39] Moltmann, *The Church*, pp. 119–21.

the presence of Christ are not correlated with the notion of friendship as much as they might be.[40]

James Nelson offers a third set of insights into the nature of
friendship. For him, friendships confirm, confront and celebrate,
though he places the greatest emphasis upon celebration.[41] In a
similar way to Rita Nakashima Brock, Nelson identifies a crucial
erotic element in friendship: 'our friendships, when they are
deep and sustained, personal and significant, have a great deal
of eroticism to them.'[42] He is speaking here of the extent and
depth of connectedness between people. Only out of such a
depth of communion are confirmation, confrontation and celebration possible. Nelson concludes: 'in the experience of the
depths of friendship with another human being, I literally do
experience the friendship of God. It is not an experience somehow "like" God . . . It *is* God.'[43] Also called 'the Christic experience', which Nelson claims Jesus had no desire to keep to
himself, this divine depth of human friendship is a kind of continuing incarnation. It is in such forms of relationship that God
is found enfleshed.

Nelson's is one of the clearest statements of the divine
significance of friendship. When viewed christologically, his
wording invites the question: is, then, friendship of a certain kind
and quality identical with Christ? In the light of our brief discussion of Moltmann's reading of friendship, we are left with the
challenge that friendships which *are* Christ, or God, will not leave
a definition of 'church' untouched. However, reference to 'the
Christic experience' is, in my view, unhelpful. Such a term so

---

[40] To give just one example: while Moltmann's helpful exploration of the division
between the dogmatic and the ethical in his discussion of 'Christ's Presence in
the Poor' should be applauded, he does not begin to wrestle with the concrete
complexities of what it might mean to respect the presence of Christ in the poor,
through being a 'friend of the poor'. Challenging Moltmann's definition of
friendship with Allan's invites theological interpreters to touch on territory
familiar, for example, to all church-workers in materially poor areas, who often
feel their cultural difference, if not in strict terms of material wealth, then at least
in terms of their ease of mobility. What possibility exists of equality and reciprocity in such settings? What, then, does the joint celebration of Christ, in open
friendship, actually mean?

[41] Nelson, *Intimate Connection*, p. 65

[42] Nelson, *Intimate Connection*, p. 54

[43] Nelson, *Intimate Connection*, p. 66 (Nelson's emphasis).

detaches an understanding of Christ from the concreteness of experience, that there is the danger of idealizing Christ.[44] It can also loosen the link between Christian understandings of Christ and the narratives about Jesus, in relation to which, as was shown in Chapter 2, all Christian explorations of Christ have to be worked out.

A Christology of friendship

The search for a Christology of friendship, through the human experience of friendship, is based on the simple perception that it is through human inter-relationship that the deepest dimensions of reality are encountered: what forgiveness, joy, the sharing of sorrow, the seeking of justice, growth, self-discovery actually are. As already noted, these are also learned through family and kinship ties. I noted also that in their exploration of God's presence and activity, churches have struggled to move beyond parent–child patterns of relationship in fashioning corporate, God-centred lives, and in fostering relations between their members. A shift to a Christology of friendship is one small contribution towards the finding of new images for God, and new ways of grasping how God in Christ is revealed in and through human relationships.

There is, admittedly, a challenge to any switch from family to friendship in Christian thinking. In his incisive recent critique of the current Christian trend towards the idolization of the family, Rodney Clapp refers to the 'erratic constellation of friends' who provide support to families. He notes also that both family and friendship 'are now increasingly regulated and controlled via the terms of the market'.[45] He is surely right to observe and to express a concern about the absence of coherence and structure in many of our current patterns of living. In his church-driven model, however, I think that he overlooks both the extent to which churches themselves are not immune to the influence of the market, and the strength and structure to living which the

---

[44] In the sense of rendering Christ only as an idea, a mental construct informing human practice.
[45] Clapp, *Families*, p. 49.

apparently erratic constellation of friends and friendships provide.[46]

Clapp would no doubt want to argue that friendship is not a
wholly good model for church. Without some form of
qualification about the limits of friendship Clapp is surely right.
Christ is not just for people of the same age or social class.
Friendships do cross age and class boundaries, but outside of
families do so often only with difficulty. To the degree that
churches are a form of social living which can bring together radically different people who might not choose each other as
friends, across many generations, churches can be a challenge to
Christologies approached both through family imagery and
friendships. But the force of some of Jesus' most difficult recorded
sayings (Matt. 8.21–22; 10.21–22; 10.34–39; Mark 3.31–35) should
not lead us simply towards understandings of church which happen to make the easiest sense in the present. Other possible mean-
ings of Jesus' words need to be explored. Clapp is surely right to
reassert the contemporary significance of the biblical concept of
covenant in his exposition. But it could be argued that such a concept finds its most obvious contemporary echo in friendship
rather than church. It may, then, be out of friendship that an
understanding of the presence of God in Christ – among friends
– can best begin.

The challenges of approaching Christology through friendship
are enormous. The equality and interdependence found in friendship provide opportunity for critique of any easy reading of Jesus
as friend gained through the 'what a friend we have in Jesus' tradition of spirituality.[47] 'Jesus' does not cease to be the figure
through which one refers to the accessibility of God in prayer, and
with whom one shares joys and sorrows. But if the friendship of
Jesus is truly reflected in – and if Nelson is right, even identified

---

[46] On this, see especially the recent observation by S. Ringe: 'In the dominant culture of North America, at least in the modern age, the category of friendship
risks trivialization and sentimentalization. In the popular perception, friends fall
into a chasm between calls for a return to "family values" and the quest to network and make business-related "contacts"' (*Wisdom's Friends: Community and
Christology in the Fourth Gospel*, Louisville: Westminster John Knox, 1999, p. 3).

[47] Especially where such a spirituality is not integrally linked with a communal
experience of Christ, or fails to see friendship in terms of full mutuality and critical challenge.

with – the deepest of friendships enjoyed by human beings, then the same notions of equality, reciprocity and interdependence found in such friendships derive from Christ, because they are located in Christ. We may even say that Christ depends on us, communally. Only through friendships – or through relationships like them – can Christ be discovered. Here we have a pointer to the existence and presence of Christ as a 'social network' of just, fulfilling, stretching, challenging relationships. We are, in short, back with the perception that Christ is a community of practice: in this case, communities that practise friendship.

Yet, one objection to the discernment of the presence of God in Christ in and through human friendship is the fact that friendships are freely chosen. The social forms of family and church differ from friendships because they are not chosen as directly. We may choose a church to which we belong, but we cannot choose who is in it. Friendships are more within our control. Arguably, perceiving Christ's presence in friendships makes Christ too subject to human wills and wishes. The hospitality of Christ to the stranger, and in the form of the stranger, is less likely to be at the fore of a Christology developed through friendship.

This is an important objection and serves as a reminder that churches that stress friendship, and conduct programmes of 'friendship evangelism', can miss the mark if they do not carefully qualify their language. Recognizing that Christ is the friend of all can lead to a failure to address how friendships actually work, and how hard they can sometimes be to form and sustain. It is profoundly difficult to develop and maintain human relationships that genuinely and consistently promote mutuality, reciprocity, solidarity, equality, openness, supportive critique and celebration.

Talk of Christ's 'friendship with all' is understandable in so far as the God who befriends is available to all in and through the figure of Jesus. However, participating in Christ through friendships may imply that Christ is only 'similar to me' or 'my kind of person'. It is for this reason that the unchosen nature of families and churches (and work and educational groups) points out a limitation of friendships as a social form of Christ. All of the different social forms in and through which God in Christ is present, and the mutual critique at work between them, are seen to be necessary.

This should not cause us to overlook what attention to friendship helps us to appreciate about Christ, which other social forms may not. At their best, friendships have no time for superficiality or avoidance, both of which easily become part of church and family life. To give some examples: though confession and absolution are an intrinsic part of the church's liturgical life, the full impact of that ritual practice may not be felt as keenly as when regret and remorse, and resolution to amend life, happen as a result of deep, soul-searching conversations between friends. And though families are a context in which the most intense joy and sadness occur, the real depth of feeling experienced on the occasion of a birth or a death is often not expressed among family members, whereas it is spoken about among friends.

Christ is thus already present among friends, at work in the loyalty, solidarity, openness, generosity, honesty and mutuality that friendship can embody and exhibit, desiring to be identified. At their best, though, churches can be societies of friends. It is to churches that we now turn.

The church as witness to Christ's body in the world

Finally we turn to the fifth (and in many ways the most obvious) social form in which God in Christ is present in the world today: the church. It is the most obvious because Christian theological tradition has made so much of the reality and concept of church. Building on words from the apostle Paul (1 Cor. 12.27), the church has been called 'the body of Christ' throughout Christian history. So why do I turn to the church only at this late stage? I certainly do not wish to suggest that we have somehow reached the crown and pinnacle of social forms of Christ, to which all other such forms are subservient, or from which all others derive. Nor am I implying that church is an afterthought, or relatively unimportant. There are three reasons for leaving exploration of the church till now.

First, in Christian tradition, so much attention has been paid to the church as a social form that we have run the risk of interpreting Christ in the light of the institution rather than vice versa. It is this tendency which I have labelled 'ecclesiocentrism', a distortion of the attempt to do theology christocentrically.[48]

Delaying my consideration of the church as a social form has been a way of trying to avoid this distortion.

Second, I have wanted to explore other ways of resisting the individualism which has caused problems in recent Christian theology. The resurgence of interest in the doctrine of the church in recent years has, in part, been an important corrective to an individualism in Christian theology brought on by some of the forms of Christian existentialism and theological liberalism that proved influential in the West throughout the 1960s and 1970s. During the same period, academic theological enquiry was also relatively detached from Christian practice (e.g. of worship). But, as increasing attention has again been paid to practice and attempts have been made to reconnect academy and church, so there has been a renewed emphasis on the doctrine of the church itself.

Allied with the resurgence of interest in the doctrine of the Trinity, this new form of attention to the church may overemphasize the social form of Christ as church.[48] I have therefore wanted to look elsewhere first for social forms in which Christ can be deemed present (hence the explorations of work, education, family and friendships).[50] Third, I have already dwelt on the relationship and tension between 'Christ' and 'church' in discussing the work of Schleiermacher, Brock and Bonhoeffer.[51] Each of those thinkers wrestled in their own way with the question of how the church must in some sense be considered to *be* Christ. At the heart of each theologian's thought, however, was an insight that demanded greater attention. Granted that church will be identifiable as a concrete, social form of Christ today, each recognized that this was not saying enough. For Schleiermacher, the

---

[48] Marsh, *Christ in Focus*, pp. 60–1.

[49] On resurgent trinitarianism, see, for example, Marsh, *Christ in Focus*, pp. 71–4.

[50] An autobiographical example may illustrate the point. I have spent much of my time in recent years switching between the social contexts of family, church (local), academy (teaching and academic seminars and conferences) and church (national, via working parties and the like). In the third and fourth cases there are always many references to ideal church. Much of my time has, however, been spent wrestling with the tension between the first two social forms of living, and the question of how God in Christ is present and active there. I shall comment more on this in the Epilogue below.

[51] On Schleiermacher, see *Christ in Focus*, ch. 4, esp. pp. 92 and 102–4; on Brock, ch. 6, esp. pp. 161–4 and 166; on Bonhoeffer, see above Chapter 1, esp. pp. 5–7 and 11–16.

heart of the matter *was* a quality of blessed fellowship which participation in Christ would bring about. Brock's focus was upon the nature of relationships that liberate, on the basis of which it would prove possible to conceive of church quite differently from the way it is conceived in much traditional theology. For Bonhoeffer, it would be necessary to look beyond the identifiable church at other social forms in which Christ must be seen to be present. His focus was more institutional and sociological than Brock's. It is as a consequence of my studies of Schleiermacher, Bonhoeffer, Brock and also Rauschenbusch that I have focused on work, education, family and friendships in order to explore where Christ is participated in, and 'practised'.

The emphasis must therefore be less upon the church as such, than on the interplay between Christ understood as present in the social form 'church' and Christ understood as present equally in the other identified forms. 'Church' remains a crucial social form, but is kept in a limited place, lest it be idolized. What, though, is the church's specific contribution to the task of identifying and participating in Christ? Granted that the being of the church is itself a social form of Christ, what more can be said?

Church as local

First, the church needs to be highlighted in its *local* manifestation. Christ is too easily kept at a distance when emphasis is placed more upon the universal church or the communion of saints. So much of what has been explored throughout this book – the presence of God and Christ in the context of real, concrete human relationships – is simply avoided when the universal church is prioritized over the local. This does not mean that the universal is unimportant, or becomes but a collection of local churches. Rather, it is being recognized that the universal church and the orthodoxy that it strives to maintain carry little significance unless a believer lives out their adherence to church and faith in concrete, local form.

Expressed in starkest form: a Christian inevitably has to be a member of some form of local group of Christians. The nature of Christian belonging is admittedly undergoing considerable change. This is due to changing patterns of church membership caused by social mobility and the lack of cultural awareness which often occurs in local church life.[52] For some Christians in the West today Christian belonging does not take the form of straightforward membership of a local church as traditionally understood.[53] However, participation in Christ must take place in some conscious ecclesial form; otherwise one important dimension of participation is lost. Discovery of, and participation in, Christ through the intensity of human relationships depends on involvement in multiple communities of practice. At least one of these needs to be a group whose explicit purpose is to help people encounter and reflect on Christ.

Churches as intentional communities

Second, therefore, the *intentionality* of church life is crucial. Of all the social forms of Christ that have been considered, the church is the one that explicitly seeks to embody Christ. Indeed, when it fails to do this, it has lost its reason for being. The church is thus the community of practice that aims to practise Christ in all that it does. It fails, of course. But in what it seeks to be and do, a church tries to do all the good things identified in Chapter 2. And as a whole, the church – in all of its many and diverse local manifestations – endeavours to be a collection of communities which mirror all the good practices that occur in work, education, families and friendships. And it does this in the name of Christ, seeking to be a form of Christ.

This intentionality has a knock-on effect. As well as attempting to do all the good things that other formative communities achieve at their best, churches offer resources through which their participants can live the whole of their lives in a christologically informed way.

---

[52] Especially the frequent lack of awareness of popular culture so that Christians feel they have to live in a number of different cultural worlds, where 'church culture' is the most out of touch with what is experienced, or participated in, for much of life.

[53] I do think this is regrettable, but it is a fact of life for many Christians, whose 'church' in the sense of theological stimulus may be more virtual, and whose participation in Christ may be more through work or education and friendships than 'church' in a traditional form. In this sense, this present study provides a theological basis for such a Christian lifestyle.

As a collection of many communities in one, the church interprets what goes on elsewhere. Though it may fail to do what it sets out to do, it invites its members, and those willing to listen to what it has to say, to reflect on the whole of life, using the theological resources that its various and diverse communities offer. Here the interplay between the church and other social forms of Christ is crucial. For the church is not claiming to be all that Christ can be. Families, friendships, work and educational groups may actually *be* Christ better. But the church's job is to help the whole of society recognize that this is so, and why this matters.

The church interprets its own life, yet also contributes to wider society. As a theological guardian of the narratives about Jesus, the church seeks to ensure that the Bible continues to be read not only as a literary or historical document. It does not undertake its theological task in isolation, for it does its work best when in constant dialogue with academy and society.[54] But it has a specific calling to be theological. It reads and rereads the story of the people of God, filtered and reinterpreted through the story of Christ, in relation to its own imperfect life; and, in so doing, it discovers more and more about who and what God in Christ is and is doing. In turn, it becomes easier for the church to say, as appropriate, of working practices and educational initiatives, or of particular patterns of family life and friendships, 'Yes, you are doing it better than we are, and you have shown us by your actions that that's clearly where Christ is too.'

The church also interprets the whole of life through its ritual practices (e.g. baptism and Holy Communion). It is imperative that the church, being a community of the Word, is not viewed merely as a community of words. Interpreting the Bible as scripture is a key part of the church's life. But its task is not confined to speaking about where Christ is found, either within its own life or in other social forms of human existence. In and through its own embodiment of Christ it also provides non-verbal signs which can be celebrated as the being and activity of God in Christ.

In its sacramental life, the church practises what it means to be in Christ through rituals which bind those who participate in them not simply to the group of people known as 'church'.

---

[54] And churches need other churches even in the theological task.

Baptism denotes being included within Christ's identifiable body in the world, belonging to Christ through membership of the church. But baptism also challenges both the baptized, and those not baptized, to consider what it means to be a baptized person in the world. In Holy Communion, the church 'joyfully celebrates the presence of Christ in its midst, calls to mind his sacrifice and, in the power of the Holy Spirit, is united with him as the Body of Christ'.[55] But participation in Holy Communion affects the whole of the lives of those who take part. As a 'fore-taste of the heavenly banquet prepared for all people',[56] Holy Communion asks questions of the eating habits of those who participate. Do they over-eat? What is their contribution to the sharing of the world's resources? Do they eat fairly traded produce? What is their practice of hospitality to others? In short, in what ways do their everyday habits anticipate the vision of all being fed, and being satisfied? Being dismissed 'to live and work to God's praise and glory' at the end of a celebration of Holy Communion is itself a challenge to every participant to do justice, to love mercy, and to walk humbly before God in the whole of their lives.[57] It is a reminder that the meaning of being 'in Christ' is far from contained within the liturgical gathering of Christ's body.

Non-verbal communication of what it means to be 'in Christ' occurs in and through the life of the church in other ways too. Brett Webb-Mitchell has explored many dimensions of this in his helpful study *Christly Gestures: Learning to be Members of the Body of Christ*.[58] Building on the extensive and widely influential work of Christian virtue ethicists such as Stanley Hauerwas, his book stresses how the church as a community cultivates particular dispositions in its members. In my view, he overstresses the church's need to structure and shape these dispositions. His approach comes close at times to that of 'heavy shepherding', which has

---

[55] *Methodist Worship Book*, Peterborough: Methodist Publishing House, 1999, p. 114.

[56] *Methodist Worship Book*, p. 197.

[57] *Methodist Worship Book*, p. 197 (cf. also, e.g., 'Be . . . fervent in the work of God's kingdom', p. 128; 'Go in joy and peace to love and serve the Lord', p. 173; 'We go into the world in the power of the Spirit to fulfil our high calling as servants of Christ', p. 184).

[58] B. P. Webb-Mitchell, *Christly Gestures: Learning to be Members of the Body of Christ*, Grand Rapids and Cambridge: Eerdmans, 2003.

proved so costly in the church's recent history.[59] But his work is important in its drawing attention to the many, often hidden, ways in which people are shaped by Christian practice. Churches are formative communities which prepare people for life, and enable them to live life better.

Rather than demonstrate how a religious life can be the structure of a meaningful life in the world, and accept their role of expounding a thoughtful, tenable theological basis upon which such a structure can be based, churches have often become 'total institutions'.[60] By contrast, I have been seeking to explore throughout this study the way in which the church takes its appropriate, interpretative place within a variety of social forms of existence in and through which God in Christ struggles to be present and active in the contemporary world.

Webb-Mitchell's work remains an important challenge to the church to consider how it can play even this interpretative role. How can it enable its members to see themselves as 'in Christ', both in and beyond the identifiable church? How can it enable its members to find a 'shape of living' which does *not* suck the whole of life into an ecclesial form, so that life is lived 'for church' in the sense that the whole of one's existence revolves around 'church activities'? How can that shape of living itself be genuinely missiological in character, not in the sense that a believer brings Christ *from* church *to* the world, but rather by the believer's seeking to celebrate, with believer and non-believer alike, where Christ in social form already is?

These are demanding tasks, both for the church as an institution and for its individual members. In my view, however, they are more appropriate kinds of demand than that of a 'heavy shepherding' approach to church life. Church growth evidence suggests that churches are not successful when they do not demand very much of people – for this implies that having faith or belonging to a Christian community does not make

[59] Like many contemporary writers, Webb-Mitchell majors on catechesis and ritual (*Christly Gestures*, chs. 6 and 8). Such emphases are important correctives to a laissez-faire kind of Protestantism which has often paid insufficient attention to structures of education and formation in the Christian life. But reading his text made me feel that an over-structured prescription was being offered.
[60] The term 'total institution' is borrowed from sociologist Erving Gofmann.

much difference to life. But invitations to people to commit themselves to a Christian way of life merely distort what it means to live such a life if they result in a summons to ecclesiastical hyperactivity, producing ecclesiomaniacs who spend all their waking hours in, or worrying about, church affairs. Christocentric Christianity as evidenced in the variety of social forms in which God in Christ is present and active in society will, at its best, have none of this.

The church thus remains a body of Christ. But we must no longer see it as *the* body of Christ. For we have always known that Christ's body is broken in and for the world. And in that case, why have we only ever tended to see this brokenness in terms of the church's disunity? Christ's broken body reflects the brokenness of humanity; and thus the imperfect way in which the church anticipates the coming reign of God is matched by the ways in which God in Christ struggles for presence in other social forms outside the church. In Christian perspective, Christians discern the presence of Christ through using their christological lens. But Christians claim too much when they see in their churches *the* body of Christ. We need to be more honest and open about what we claim to see, but recognize its partiality (in both senses). What we see is limited, and it is particular. But we do claim to see God at work, and God, as far as we are concerned, is always Christ-like. From the perspective of 'church' we also claim to be able to see how God is present and at work in Christ in work, education, families and friendships too. But those social forms of Christ in turn tell us much. The church is, then, ultimately *a witness* to the body of Christ in the world, and not *the* body of Christ. It seems to me that such a conclusion is fully in keeping with what Paul, not even a regular member of any local church, meant when he said to a group of Corinthians, 'you are the body of Christ'. Despite the way that that text has been interpreted and used, it need not be understood in an exclusive manner.

And what of Christ in all of this (once more)?

What does such an exploration of Christ through family, friendships and church enable us to see about who and what Christ is?

The Lordship of Christ revisited

The first conclusion is that Christ's 'Lordship' needs careful hand-ling. It is common knowledge that 'Jesus is Lord' was probably the earliest Christian confession.[61] For the first Christians, in the context of the Roman Empire, the statement meant, at the very least and often to their cost, that they were refusing to worship the emperor and choosing to worship Jesus as God instead. Within four centuries, the Lordship of Christ had come to mean that Jesus the Christ was like an emperor, and an image of him could adorn the apex of a basilica.[62] As Lord of all, the cosmic Christ, he looked down on the whole world. This was, surely, what 'God-likeness', or even 'being God', must mean. But the nagging persistence of those canonical gospel narratives through Christian history, and the findings of this chapter, suggest that respect for the Lordship of Christ may not be best expressed in human affairs in terms of imperial or cosmic power. 'God above' may be important as poetic language, in maintaining respect for God's transcendent otherness, but it misleads if it prevents our seeing that being 'in Christ' draws us much more towards mutu-ality, equality and solidarity and the often intense relationships in which such qualities emerge. This is the lesson taught by experi-ence of family-like life, friendships and even, at its best, what it means to be church.

Clearly there will be a marked difference in how Christ and 'being in Christ' are construed depending on which of the rela-tionships explored in this chapter proves dominant in the chris-tological exploration undertaken. Start within a family with a child's relationship to a parent and being in Christ could take 'Lordship' as 'Fatherhood'. Start with a friendship, and 'Lord-

---

[61] On this, see, for example, the work of L. W. Hurtado, *One God One Lord: Early Christian Devotion and Ancient Jewish Monotheism*, London: SCM Press, 1988, and now, more extensively, *Lord Jesus Christ: Devotion to Jesus in Earliest Christianity*, Grand Rapids: Eerdmans, 2003.

[62] On the development of visual images of Jesus in Christian history, see, for exam-ple, D. Thomas, *The Face of Christ*, London, New York, Sydney, Toronto: Hamlyn, 1979, J. Pelikan, *Jesus through the Centuries*, London and New Haven: Yale University Press, 1985, and R. Harries, 'Art' in J. L. Houlden (ed.), *Jesus in History, Thought and Culture: An Encyclopedia Vol. 1*, Santa Barbara, Denver; Oxford: ABC Clio, 2003, pp. 66–106.

ship' looks puzzling, but might mean 'allegiance' or 'alliance'. Start with 'church' and it is sometimes difficult to look beyond a church's patterns of ministry, denoting the way in which a church organizes its life, for how it interprets the Lordship of Christ. But not all family life is patriarchal, and the church is not defined by its ministries. This chapter has sought to disclose many ways in which mutuality, solidarity, equality and hospitality (and all those other good things which families and friendships at their best inspire and embody) can be respected without our being sentimental, unrealistic and politically naive.

All that is good in families and friendships must inform the way we understand the Lordship of Christ. To call Jesus the Christ 'Lord' commits the one who makes the confession to living in, and to fostering, the types of relationships that inspire mutuality, solidarity and so on. Jesus Christ is Lord, and therefore the corporate nature of church life matters more than its patterns of ministry. Jesus Christ is Lord, and therefore even in families, where hierarchies inevitably form in some way, mutual respect must still hold sway. Jesus Christ is Lord, and therefore honest, searching, forgiving, demanding friendships become the norm of human relationships. Jesus Christ is Lord, and therefore wherever hierarchies do form in human life, they are judged by whether or not they ascribe rank and status to those within them. Where the ascribing of rank takes over, then respect for the Lordship of Christ as found in the narratives about Jesus in the canonical Gospels disappears.

Christ and Kingdom

Second, this chapter has accentuated the conceptual and temporal space between the reign of God as now is and the reign of God to come. Or, to express this differently, being bodies of Christ in the world and witnesses to the one body of Christ helps those who participate in Christ to see the importance of the insight that Christ is yet to come. As an eschatological movement within Judaism, the first Christians (not called such at first) believed that with Jesus 'the end' had somehow come. They still looked forward, though. For Jesus himself taught and, in many of his actions, brought into the here and now a reign of God which remained largely in the future. Yet what was happening around Jesus – the very words and actions which made his closest followers call him 'Christ' – created the sense that this was 'the end'. Every example of evil being countered, of the unwell or the unpopular being included once more within society, of compassion or of wealth-sharing was like the end – God's hoped-for future – coming into being now.

To call the church alone the body of Christ is to tame and localize inappropriately the coming of the reign of God. For if the reign of God resists institutionalization (it remains ever a vision to be acted out, performed, in myriad ways), then it cannot be adequately contained in any single form. 'Body of Christ' is a powerful and essential concept to enable us to denote how and where the reign of God is already breaking in: if the reign of God is not to remain abstract, then we must show where it is concretely present. It resists institutionalization, but it must take concrete shape. This is the tension between the 'not yet' and the 'already' of the reign of God.

However, Christ is not only present as church. Therefore the body of Christ is broken across humanity: 'we human beings are a fragmented race. We are human beings but not yet humanity: we are not yet a human people.'[63] Christ's body is thus the new humanity, approaching us in visionary form from God's future, but currently broken, awaiting fulfilment, and in the meantime struggling to find form among us, as church, yes, but in other forms too.

---

[63] McCarthy, *Sex and Love*, p. 149.

7 'God be in my head': On participating in the mind of Christ

'It matters more than anything in the world that the narrative of God's dealings with humankind should be imprinted on the physic and chemistry of the human brain.'[1]

At the end of the long investigation conducted across *Christ in Focus* and this present book, one central question remains. What goes on in the Christian's head in the light of all this? Supplementary questions then emerge. Is the brain-functioning that significant? Is this too rational an approach to how a religious faith works? What of recent theories of mind which have challenged the 'ghost in the machine' approach to human physiology? Does not a 'communities of practice' approach undermine much of what has gone on under the name of 'Christian spirituality'? For has not the focus of Christian spirituality been shifted from the inner life to what goes on between people? And is a 'communities of practice' approach to Christology and Christian living workable anyway? If Christology is how Christians do their God-thinking and their God-talk, does it really affect how they do their jobs, their studies and their relating to friends and family members? Does not the notion of 'participating in Christ' end up as some kind of fantasy in which a proportion of human beings happen to live (while others live within different fantasies)? What difference does it all make?

These questions set the agenda for this final chapter and for the brief Epilogue which follows it. This chapter concludes the theological enquiry by opening up its findings in the direction of spirituality. In the same way that I find no clear distinction between

[1] S. Sykes, 'Ritual and the Sacrament of the Word' in D. Brown and A. Loades (eds), *Christ the Sacramental Word: Incarnation, Sacrament and Poetry*, London: SPCK, 1996, pp.157–67, here p. 167.

systematic and practical theology, so I am not separating practical theology and spirituality. But at this point in the study I must simply state how all that has been explored takes effect in the mind and experience of the individual believer. (And what do we mean by 'mind' anyway?)

Discerning 'the mind of Christ'

There is frequent reference to 'the mind of Christ' in Christian spirituality. Christians today often pick up what Paul says in his letters to early Christians as he wrestles with what it means to relate to Christ. It is of profound significance in his view that Christians 'have the mind of Christ' (1 Cor. 2.16). Offering *nous* in Greek (mind) as his rendering of Isaiah 40.3, when citing the Septuagint version of that text ('For who has known the mind of the Lord . . .?'), Paul knows that the answer can only be 'no one'. And yet participation in the spirit of Christ is as good as knowing Christ's 'mind'. The linguistic slipperiness is telling, however. In selecting the term *nous* Paul has opted to use a word to do with reason and intellect. Yet it can also mean 'intuition'. And when he switches with ease between 'spirit' and 'mind', this indicates that having the mind of Christ will not simply be a rational process.

Nous also appears in an important passage in Romans. In Paul's view, the mind (*nous*) of a follower of Jesus Christ is transformed (Rom. 12.2) in a way which affects the whole person, for bodies too are to be 'holy and acceptable to God' (Rom. 12.1). It does admittedly look as though Paul implies that the 'mind' (or 'spirit', we must assume) takes the lead in the process of transformation.[2] Bodies are to be presented as holy and acceptable, but this apparently occurs as a result of the mind's transformation.

---

[2] Discussion around the complexities of Paul's anthropological (and related) terms has raged for decades and will not be solved here. Important studies on this topic include: J. A. T. Robinson, *The Body*, London: SCM Press, 1952; R. Jewett, *Paul's Anthropological Terms*, Leiden: Brill, 1971; H. J. Eckstein, *Der Begriff Syneidesis bei Paulus: Eine neutestamentlich-exegetische Untersuchung zum Gewissensbegriff*, Tübingen: J. C. B. Mohr (Paul Siebeck), 1983. For a recent treatment, see, for example, relevant sections of J. D. G. Dunn, *The Theology of Paul the Apostle*, Grand Rapids: Eerdmans, 1997. Whether dualistic in this thinking or not, there can be little doubt of his conviction of the fundamental interconnectedness of body, mind and spirit.

The transformation of the person, however, even if led by the mind's/spirit's transformation, is clearly dependent upon a person's being included 'in Christ'. As Barrett suggests, Paul uses the word *nous* in a markedly different way from other Greek writers, for whom the mind is usually assumed to be good.[3] In Romans 12.2, in contrast to others writing in Greek at the time, the need for the mind's renewal is emphasized. Reason thus has its place in the task of discerning Christ. It is part of what 'mind' means. But it is a renewed, transformed reason which can discern more than would be possible by the application of intellectual faculties alone.

Perhaps the most influential of all have been Paul's words of introduction to the christological hymn in Philippians 2.5: 'Let the same mind be in you (*phroneite*; lit.: hold an opinion, a judgement, think) that was in Christ Jesus.' This text has been very prominent in Christian thinking and living. Having 'the mind of Christ' in this context means being shaped both by the *kenosis* (self-emptying) and the *exaltation* of Jesus Christ the servant. The Philippians are to be at one with each other, and they will be so if they respect the fact that they are 'in Christ Jesus'. Christian living is not, then, a matter of discerning the mind of Jesus Christ (rationally or otherwise) and then trying to copy him. It is more a matter of discovering what it means to participate in Christ. Participation in Christ brings all that Paul has described in Philippians 2.2–4. But he then goes on to remind them, by means of a liturgical version of the Jesus story (Phil. 2.6–11), what God has been up to in Christ.

These three passages from Paul offer biblical examples of how understandings of 'the mind of Christ' have taken shape in Christian thinking and living. The phrase appears in Christian hymnody too.[4] It is prominent, for example, in the evangelical

---

[3] C. K. Barrett, *The Epistle to the Romans*, London: A & C Black, 1962, p. 233.

[4] This builds on a long-standing tradition in spirituality about being given 'the mind that was in Christ', as, for example, in Charles Wesley's hymn 'God of all power, and truth, and grace' (verse 4, 'Give me a new, a perfect heart / From doubt, and fear, and sorrow free / The mind that was in Christ impart / And let my spirit cleave to thee'), first published in 1742. Early Methodists would also sing '. . . arm yourselves with all the mind / That was in Christ, your Head' when singing Charles Wesley's 'Soldiers of Christ, arise' (first published in John Wesley's *The Character of a Methodist*, also 1742). John Wesley himself explored the theme in his 1733 sermon, 'The Circumcision of the Heart', which includes a reference to Philippians 2.5 in its final sentence (*The Works of John Wesley Volume 1, Sermons I, 1–33*, Nashville: Abingdon Press, 1984, pp. 398–414).

hymn 'May the mind of Christ my Saviour', by the English Anglican hymn-writer Kate Barclay Wilkinson (1859–1928). The first verse reads:

> May the mind of Christ my Saviour
> Live in me from day to day,
> By his love and power controlling
> All I do or say.[5]

Here, the 'mind' is clearly more than rationality. Christ's presence 'takes over' the individual believer. 'Control' is a heavy word, which would be off-putting to potential followers who might be unused to the counter-cultural approach of Christianity that resists concluding that human beings are wholly autonomous and fully 'in control' of their own destinies. It smacks of being brainwashed. In the context of a life of Christian faith, of course, and sung in the context of worship, the hymn simply reinforces the point that living Christianly means that you conduct yourself within a framework of living shaped by personal knowledge – corporately held, but individually appropriated – of a Christ-like God.

In the hymn, 'the mind of Christ' is supplemented by 'the word of God' (verse 2), 'the peace of God the Father' (verse 3), and 'the love of Jesus' (verse 4), as available resources out of which Christians can 'run the race' before them (verse 5). The believer looks 'only unto Jesus' (verse 5). This is Christocentrism made comprehensible (and singable, and thus liturgically transmittable) in terms of the daily living of the Christian individual.

A third, common use of the term 'the mind of Christ' occurs in church documents and reports. A great many of these, across all denominations, are described as resulting from the church's task to discern Christ's mind on a given topic. Examples abound. The *Catechism of the Catholic Church* notes that 'By living with the mind of Christ, Christians *hasten the coming of the Reign of God*, "a kingdom of justice, love and peace".'[6] *The Virginia Report* of the Inter-

---

[5] First published in *Golden Bells*, London: Children's Special Service Mission, 1925; now available, for example, in *Hymns and Psalms*, Peterborough: Methodist Publishing House, 1983, no. 739.

[6] *Catechism of the Catholic Church*, London: Geoffrey Chapman, 1994, para. 2046 (emphasis in original).

Anglican Theological and Doctrinal Commission (1997) states: 'Anglicans are held together by the characteristic way in which they use Scripture, tradition and reason in discerning afresh the mind of Christ for the Church in each generation.'[7] In the Second Interim Report of The Scottish Churches Initiative For Union (SCIFU, 2000), there are three references to the 'mind of Christ'. The councils of the proposed new structures are all 'responsible for prayerfully discerning the mind of Christ for the Church' (para. 9.1). In a paragraph examining whether the initiative should be seen as 'top-down', the following statement appears: 'What is crucial is that all "levels" of church life . . . prayerfully, and together, seek the mind of Christ' (para. 13.2). Finally, the report declares: 'The SCIFU group believes that the process towards union is one that has to be undertaken prayerfully, seeking the mind of Christ for the Church in Scotland today' (para. 16).[8] Many more examples could be cited.

These are expressions of every church's desire to discern the will of God in the light of Paul's insight that 'Those who are spiritual discern all things' and that 'we have the mind of Christ' (1 Cor. 2.15–16). It is 'having the mind of Christ' which enables churches to believe that it is possible for them to discern God's will. Yet there is usually an appropriate reticence, in that churches recognize that the mind of Christ itself has to be sought.[9]

What insights can be distilled from these examples of the use of the concept of the mind of Christ from scripture, liturgy and official church statements? First, it is clear that discernment of the mind of Christ is not simply a matter of rational processing. 'Mind' does not simply mean 'reason'. It is not just a case of thinking one's way, individually or collectively, towards what Christ thinks or wills. Even if rational mental processes are involved, so that the task of discernment does not produce irrational results, discernment involves more than thinking. Churches, for example, pray, discuss and listen to those who carry authority among them, when seeking the mind of Christ.

[7] *The Virginia Report: The Report of the Inter-Anglican Theological and Doctrinal Commission*, London: Anglican Consultative Council, 1997, 3.5
[8] All of the SCIFU documents can be found on the Church of Scotland's website: www.churchofscotland.org
[9] And less positively, of course, it has to be admitted that so many ecumenical disputes in effect take the form of one church declaring or implying that 'we have the mind of Christ', while others imply 'no, we do!'

Second, the mind of Christ may infuse the daily life of individuals, as the hymn cited suggests, but having the mind of Christ is not only an individual matter. The churches' discernment of the mind of Christ implies a corporate carrying of the mind of Christ, as well as a collective search for it. The mind of Christ pervades the church, as the church seeks to live within Christ. Something happens corporately in the search; not even authoritative individuals (bishops, priests, deacons, for example) might 'have' the mind of Christ any more than other individuals. Christians acting on the basis of a church's discernment of the mind of Christ then participate in a collective 'mind'. At its best, participation in the mind of Christ represents neither the dominance of any individual's particular gift of discernment nor the totalitarianism of an all-controlling institution. Participation in the mind of Christ brings life. However, to live consciously in Christ entails an inevitable tension between being an individual religious believer and being part of a community of faith to which one belongs. Individuals seeking to discern the mind of Christ will not usually view themselves independently of the collective task of discernment.

'Having' or 'discerning' the mind of Christ can thus be seen to be shorthand for seeking out God's will. But how might this tradition of Christian spirituality be affected by the enquiries conducted in this book? How might the concept of 'community of practice' and recent thinking about 'mind' alter, and even undermine, what Christians usually take 'the mind of Christ' to mean? Traditionally, God's will has somehow been held to be uniform, to be 'out there', and to need tapping into via prayer and study. Reference to 'the mind of Christ' has then meant 'accessing' this uniform divine will, via what we know of Jesus the Christ, since 'the mind of Christ' and 'the will of God' have been seen as synonymous. But today's culture is not comfortable with metaphysics of any kind, and even some Christian theologians have declared a non-foundationalist approach to knowledge to be inevitable.[10] In that case, it is no longer possible to refer to 'the

---

[10] 'Non-foundationalism' claims that there are no universally agreed criteria according to which human conversations can be had and conclusions drawn. All knowledge is thus tradition- or community-specific. In religion and theology, then, particularity is all-important and the level of difficulty attached to religious traditions trying to relate to each other becomes immense. J. E. Thiel, *Nonfoundationalism*, Minneapolis: Fortress Press, 1994, is a helpful introduction to this whole topic.

mind of Christ' as if the meaning of the phrase is clear. What it was assumed to mean may certainly not be the contemporary meaning carried by the term. If 'the will of God' is tenable as a concept in any meaningful sense, then we will have to show clearly what contribution theological reflection can offer to contemporary spirituality, in the light of recent developments in thinking about knowledge and mind.

The challenge of situated cognition: 'the mind of Christ' in contemporary perspective

Outside of theology, explorations of communities of practice have been accompanied by many assumptions, sometimes examined, often not, about mind, knowledge, learning, belonging, human being, the body and society. Recent studies of human knowledge have drawn attention to the way in which 'thinking seems to lie in the relationship between the individual and the environment', where 'environment' means physical space, history and culture.[11] 'Thus, thinking as well as knowing and remembering are thought to be *distributed phenomena* rather than residing in the head of individuals.'[12] Such an approach to thinking and knowledge is known as 'situated cognition'. Human knowledge may therefore not be confined to mere 'facts' (data to be stored cognitively in the memory banks of individuals) nor even to skills, according to which individuals know 'how to' do something on the basis of acquired knowledge. The social context in which one 'knows' something or 'knows how to do' something is also of crucial importance in the act of knowing. It is on the basis of this revised thinking about knowledge, that the concept of community of practice becomes so important.

This may admittedly sound sociologically reductionistic, as if a sociological account of what is occurring between people in social settings explains everything. It seems especially so in the following quotation:

[11] W.-M. Roth, 'Authentic School Science: Intellectual Traditions' in R. McCormick and C. Paechter (eds), *Learning and Knowledge*, London: Paul Chapman Publishing, 1999, pp. 6–20, here p. 15.
[12] Roth, 'Authentic School Science', p. 15 (my emphasis).

> From a community of practice perspective, learning is squarely located in the processes of social coparticipation, not in the heads of individuals. Rather than asking what kind of cognitive processes and structures are involved, the situated learning paradigm focuses on the kinds and quality of social engagements needed to provide optimal learning environments.[13]

Here, the clarification that learning does not take place primarily (or at all?) in the individual's head means that the 'holding' of knowledge is itself distributed.

These are important contemporary insights which are beginning to be used in Christian theology and practice. Indeed, they are very helpful for understanding how Christianity works as a religion. However, while joining those who support the value of these insights from situated cognition, I also want to oppose the implication that no learning process or knowledge acquisition goes on in the individual. I agree that no individual learns independently of multiple communities of practice, and yet stating this can underplay what goes on in the head of the individual in response to their individual participation in many communities.

In Christian terms, and with respect to the subject matter of this present study, the consequences of acknowledging value to insights gained through attention to the situated nature of cognition are clear. First, my conclusion that Christ is best studied as a corporate phenomenon – from Jesus-and-his-movement to the Christ in whom we participate – fits neatly with a situated cognition approach to knowledge and learning. Knowing Christ is primarily about participating in Christ. Having the mind of Christ means partaking in Christ's mind as that mind is shared among those who do, or seek to do, the will of God.

It will be clear by now that an ambiguity must be left at this point. Not all those who seek to 'have the mind of Christ' (and do the will of God) may necessarily prove successful. Those who may not be seeking to have the mind of Christ at all may nevertheless be doing God's will.[14] Similarly, churches may consciously be seeking the mind of Christ, yet not find it, even while trying to

---

[13] Roth, 'Authentic School Science', p. 16.
[14] Matthew's parable about the two sons has deep resonance (Matt. 21.28–32).

'inhabit' it via their practices. Other groups (e.g. in work, education, families and friendships) may not consciously be attempting to be 'in Christ' yet may participate nevertheless via their person-forming practices. Christians have no special insight to be able to adjudicate on all of this, as to who is 'really in Christ' and who not.

Second, when knowing and remembering Christ, or having the mind of Christ, are understood as 'distributed phenomena', this confirms that they are more than just rational processes undertaken by individuals. They result from participation in Christ (which is not merely the same as participation in religious practice). There is an assumption at work about what it means to *be* a person, and to *be* a Christian, when we move beyond giving attention to individual rational processes alone. This is not always recognized in the literature about situated cognition.[15] Belonging and participation *do something* to a person. It is right to claim that learning and the acquisition of knowledge are not merely cognitive events occurring in the life of the individual. But individuals are affected personally by their participation. A person *is* a participant (in Christ), *is* a learner (of and about Christ), and is bound to others in and through the person-forming communities of practice where she or he discovers who and what Christ is. To have, or to participate in, the mind of Christ is thus an experience of the whole person. It is an encounter with Christ's real presence.

Third, it is important to stress that a learner participates in multiple communities of practice. This in itself challenges any tendency towards ecclesiocentrism. Christ really is present in multiple social forms and not merely, or perhaps even primarily, in the social form in which people consciously seek the presence of, and celebrate participation in, Christ. The significance of participation in Christ in multiple social forms requires appreciation in two ways. Individuals have to respect their dependence upon the existence of many communities in which Christ takes form. Diverse communities (even churches) must accept that they are not the sole form in which Christ is present in the world. Christ's presence is not, then, precisely pinpointed or grasped by any single

---

[15] Though some accounts do move beyond reason (and address the emotions, as, for example, in the quotation from Jerome Bruner, cited above in Chapter 5 n. 39).

group. Christ is discovered in the context of the various practices of groups that contribute to the formation of human persons.

This leads directly to a fourth observation. Looking at Christ's corporate presence in multiple communities of practice, rather than at the individual's participation, emphasizes the experience of being encountered and discovered by Christ as opposed to a person finding Christ on the basis of what she or he already knows or believes. When 'knowing' is participation, being known by Christ takes priority over knowing. Such an approach to Christology therefore opposes the view that an individual first draws a conclusion, or even adopts a belief, about Christ which she or he then puts into practice or applies. Being encountered by Christ is likely to include a cognitive element, even while going beyond it for belief is always about both head and heart. But the encounter may well begin in the multidimensional challenge of the task of forming persons (others and oneself) within a variety of contexts like those examined in this book.

Christology, spirituality and communities of practice: some working conclusions

'It matters', Sykes urges, 'more than anything in the world that the narrative of God's dealings with humankind should be imprinted on the physic and chemistry of the human brain.' The same might well be said by Christians and people from other religious traditions. The questions 'which narrative'?' and 'do some or all religious traditions share the same basic story?' would then arise, but there would be no dispute about the importance and urgency of the matter.[16]

---

[16] I write these words within days of the London bombings of 7 July 2005, in the wake of which there has been widespread, thoughtful engagement with questions such as how religious traditions teach their traditions, how and why the teaching of them can 'go wrong' (tragically wrong), what it means to be 'in' a tradition (does it brainwash you?), and how societies should monitor religious teachings and practices. For commentators inclined to criticize all religions, the solution seems clear: it is religions that are themselves the problem. To people of faith, the importance of faith is equally clear, for we all live by something and within some tradition even if we pretend not to. From a theological perspective the issue is plain: you have to be part of a good (and truthful) story. It matters terribly that you are conscious of what story or stories you live within, what those stories are, and what they do to you. This is the point well made by Sykes here.

Perhaps the phrase 'imprinted on the physic and chemistry of the human brain' needs some rethinking in the light of this book's enquiry, and the content of this chapter especially. It puts the emphasis too much on the workings inside the head of an individual believer. What goes on for an individual remains crucial, of course. Christ is participated in by individuals, after all. But the sociocultural theory of mind which has informed this study suggests that the notion of 'imprinting' on an individual brain cannot sufficiently respect the complexity of divine action and presence as known in Christ. Of course, Sykes can argue that his statement comes in a chapter about liturgy. He is studying how the Christian narrative becomes part of a person, so that a believer can inhabit it, and 'live it'. Sykes's interests are, in that sense, similar to my own. Yet my approach has caused me to follow a significantly different path, while addressing the same concern.[17] I began from the question of the social forms of human existence in and through which we should expect to be able to encounter Christ. I have also drawn on what we know about learning and knowledge with respect to the social contexts in which people are formed. The result is different understandings of what it means to learn (and learn about) Christ, to carry or inhabit the narrative/tradition and to have the mind of Christ. It is advisable to think and talk less about what goes on in individual brains, and more about the complexity of intersubjectivity. 'You are who you belong to', or 'you are who you depend upon'. Christ, self and others are to be encountered and explored at a deep level wherever such human interactions occur.

In closing this study, I return to the social theorist whose work began the enquiries to which I have given a theological twist in Chapters 4 to 7. Etienne Wenger's study of communities of practice contains further useful insights which relate directly to what Christians are doing when they participate in Christ, and when they seek to communicate their understanding of that participation to others inside and outside Christian faith. Of the many concepts with which Wenger works, two are especially pertinent now: participation and reification.

---

[17] I shall offer thoughts on why I have ended up with this approach in the Epilogue below.

By 'participation' Wenger means 'the social experience of living in the world in terms of membership and active involvement in social enterprises'.[18] This definition focuses upon social realities. To correlate this with notions of participation in Christ might seem instantly to favour sociological accounts of what it means to be 'in Christ'.[19] It may seem as though other kinds of accounts of participation in Christ – those focusing more on prayer, personal faith, or individual moral conduct – would be excluded. But Wenger's exposition proves to be even more helpful:

> Participation . . . is both personal and social . . . is a complex process that combines doing, talking, thinking, feeling, and belonging . . . involves our whole person, including our bodies, minds, emotions, and social relations . . . is an active process.[20]

Though the emphasis is on social realities, Wenger's point is that the individual and the corporate, the embodied and the elusively immaterial are all interwoven.

What is more, participation is not something that we simply opt into at whim, or as a one-off occurrence as if we were making a visit to a sporting event or rock concert. Wenger's understanding is that participation in a community of practice 'is broader than mere engagement in practice'. It is 'a constituent of meaning . . . a constituent of our identities. As such, participation is not something we turn on and off.'[21]

If I use Wenger's analysis to explore what it means to 'have the mind of Christ' or to 'participate in Christ', I reach two clear conclusions. First, participation in Christ may be best understood not as belonging to a social organization in any simple sense. It

---

[18] E. Wenger, *Communities of Practice: Learning, Meaning, and Identity*, Cambridge: Cambridge University Press, p. 55.

[19] Though 'participation in Christ' is a common line of enquiry in Pauline studies, see, for example, D. E. H. Whiteley, *The Theology of St Paul*, 2nd edn, Oxford: Blackwell, 1980, where the exploration links participation with atonement and baptism. Scrutiny of Paul's 'in Christ' language often becomes examination merely of Paul's ecclesiology. This tendency is, as will be clear by now, worth a careful rethink.

[20] Wenger, *Communities of Practice*, pp. 55–6.

[21] Wenger, *Communities of Practice*, p. 57. This suggests that there is more of an ontological understanding of belonging to a community of practice than first meets the eye, even if it is not spelt out as such.

includes being part of a variety of social groups in which person-formation is occurring in a deep way. Second, participation in Christ appears to presuppose an understanding of what it means for a person to 'be', which links individual self-understanding and a strong affiliation with the community within which one participates. Such an understanding locates what it means for a human being to think and be (and thus for a person 'in Christ' to think and be, or for a person to think and be 'in Christ') firmly within a social sphere.

These two conclusions confirm the findings of the exploration conducted throughout this study. If we want to do Christian the-ological reflection, we are required to pay attention to the social forms in which Christ is present. Theologians must do justice to the way in which people are shaped through their participation of crucial, formative groups.

The second term I borrow from Wenger is 'reification'. By this he means 'the process of giving form to our experience by pro-ducing objects that congeal this experience [of participation] into "thingness"'.[22] By virtue of living we operate as human beings in all sorts of different social groupings (communities of practice). We also record and display evidence of our participa-tion in such communities in all sorts of ways. This is not simply a matter of producing whatever 'work' (in the widest sense) is required of us in such communities. Nor is it always a conscious act of community-building. But we do spend a lot of time on the activity.

> Reification occupies much of our collective energy: from entries in a journal to historical records, from poems to ency-clopaedias, from names to classification systems, from dol-mens to space probes, from the Constitution to a signature on a credit card slip, from gourmet recipes to medical proce-dures, from flashy advertisements to census data, from single concepts to entire theories, from the evening news to national archives, from lesson plans to the compilation of text-books, from private addresses to sophisticated credit reporting data-bases, from tortuous political speeches to the yellow pages. In all these cases, aspects of human experience and practice

[22] Wenger, *Communities of Practice*, p. 58.

are congealed into fixed forms and given the status of object.[23]

This striking list can be adapted when we turn to thinking about how Christ (in the form of reflection on the significance of Jesus) and participation in Christ are reified, frequently without any explicit thought as to the distinction between the two, in many concrete forms. We could say:

> Reification occupies much of our collective energy as Christians – cultural, as well as ecclesial: from jottings in devotional diaries to full accounts of the life of Jesus, from poems and hymns to dictionaries of Jesus, the Gospels and early Christianity, from christological titles to full-scale works of systematic theology, from tomb-stone inscriptions to cosmic Christologies, from TV documentaries to box-office films, from creeds to liturgical texts, from bumper stickers to church statistics, from educational syllabi to worship resources, from sermons to works of art. In all these cases, aspects of the experience and practice of participation in Christ are congealed into fixed forms, given the status of object, at the same time as it is assumed that it is Christ, rather than just us, that is being spoken about.

Christology in Christian terms: interpreting Jesus as the Christ, and thus who Christ is for us today unfolds, then, as constantly interwoven with a responsibility to interpret how and where Christ is present among human communities. Included within this is the twofold task of interpreting the records and traces of what people actually *do* with Jesus the Christ, and interpreting what forms of human community may count as evidence of the presence of Christ in the world. The reification of Christ in such forms as those just listed gives us clues to who, what and where Christ is. This will inevitably lead us to forms of church, though not exclusively so. We must respect also the multiple communities of practice in and through which God in Christ seeks presence.

One further aspect of reificiation is worth noting: 'Reification shapes our experience.'[24] The very existence of all these con-

---

[23] Wenger, *Communities of Practice*, p. 59.
[24] Wenger, *Communities of Practice*, p. 59.

crete forms in which Christ is available in our culture affects who we are and what we do.[25] This insight correlates well with the emphases of narrative theology and post-liberalism, which have stressed the way in which people 'inhabit' a story (the Christian story, or the story of Christ) through participation in some form of Christian community. All of Wenger's emphases, in other words (community, practice, participation and reification) reveal themselves to be wholly contemporary and continuous with some current movements in theology.[26] What Wenger's insights add to the discussion at this point, it seems to me, is the *extent and variety* of the forms that we should be considering, which contribute to our understanding of the reified form of Christ.[27] Narrative theology and post-liberalism could, in other words, be accused of not being culturally astute enough in discerning how the story/stories that people live within are constructed.

So the cluster of terms I have been examining ('being in Christ', 'having the mind of Christ', 'participating in Christ') are clarified in at least two respects by considering the work of the social theorist Etienne Wenger. His use of the term 'participation' has helped us focus on the all-absorbing nature of involvement, and

---

[25] The 'we' here can mean Christians or human beings, depending on the extent to which we read this statement in intra-ecclesial terms. There are two issues which ideally need taking further here: (1) whether 'Christ' could be said to be available in reified forms beyond the ways in which Jesus the Christ is interpreted and offered across many cultures (e.g. as 'Christ figures' in literature and film); (2) the question of the extent to which, and ways in which, those beyond Christianity are genuinely shaped/allow themselves to be shaped by reified forms of Jesus the Christ.

[26] And this has its good and bad aspects. It is good because it is current. It is bad because it is possible to see that theological fashion may move on.

[27] In this respect, Wenger's work fits in well with the work, for example, of David Morgan and Colleen McDannell, both of whom look at the popular, material forms in which religious ideas are 'carried' in (especially Protestant) culture. It also connects with the work of those who want a much more prominent role for popular culture to interweave with the work of theologians (e.g. Tom Beaudoin, Alex Wright, Gordon Lynch). Interestingly, some of these calls come from people not connected with churches, yet who still find an essential role for theology. This is a major challenge to much of the way that theology is done and is to be done. How, in other words, is the broad cultural reification of Christ to be welcomed and used theologically in a way which does not simply re-assert a place for the church in any old 'Christendom' sense, but which may yet have to find a new way of speaking of the social form/s of Christianity?

the social dimension of the group in which one is involved. 'Reification' helps in the task of identifying the many and diverse ways in which Jesus the Christ is presented in culture/s. When people fashion images of Jesus they are always doing more than presenting or interpreting him. They are reflecting something of the person-forming function that narratives about Jesus have, and have always had, in human culture.[28]

'Being in Christ', 'participating in Christ' and 'having the mind of Christ' mean 'practising Christ'.[29] But to practise Christ in the light of the enquiry conducted here needs a closer definition of 'practise'. Here is Wenger again:

> The concept of practice connotes doing, but not just doing in and of itself. It is doing in a historical and social context that gives structure and meaning to what we do. In this sense, practice is always social practice . . . Such a concept of practice includes both the explicit and the tacit. It includes what is said and what is left unsaid; what is represented and what is assumed.[30]

This rich definition invites fuller exploration than can be offered here. Against any tendency to subsume practice within 'sheer activity' (or in the case of churches, mere 'events' – even 'worship events'), Wenger offers a more reflective, social understanding. He goes further:

> The term *practice* is sometimes used as an antonym for theory, ideas, ideals, or talk. However, my use of the term does not reflect a dichotomy between the practical and the theoretical, ideals and reality, or talking and doing. Communities of practice include all of these.[31]

---

[28] I have touched on this question via examination of the multiple agendas at work in the Quest of the Historical Jesus in 'Diverse Agendas at Work in the Jesus Quest' in T. Holmen and S. Porter (eds), *Handbook of the Study of the Historical Jesus: Vol. II*, Leiden: Brill (forthcoming 2006).

[29] And other more familiar phrases could be drawn on at this point too: 'learning Christ', 'growing into Christ', 'practising the presence of Christ', and even 'imitating Christ'.

[30] Wenger, *Communities of Practice*, p. 47.

[31] Wenger, *Communities of Practice*, p. 48.

'The practice of Christ' is thus not a method (as in 'methodism'[32]), nor a set of unreflective activities; nor is it even being the church (though, as noted in Chapter 6, the church is needed as a witness to Christ).[33] It is a way of being, certainly, and could, then, be held to be about 'being Christian'. But this 'being Christian' is not a solitary venture, and will need to be understood in a way that will continue to relate to 'church' while also challenging easy equations of churchgoing, church affiliation, moral endeavour and the notion of 'being in Christ'. Furthermore, it stands in stark contrast to understandings of 'having the mind of Christ' that would stress the personal faith or private devotion and spirituality of the individual. This understanding of 'being in Christ' as 'practising Christ' thus invites theologians to work at what social theories of mind might do to our thinking.

It seems to me that exploring the meaning/s of 'being in Christ', 'having the mind of Christ' and 'participating in Christ' helps us not only to think about being Christian but also to debate generally what it means to be human in community today. This is as it should be. For in Christ, the new humanity has come. At the end of his stimulating study *Sex and Love in the Home: A Theology of the Household*, David Matzko McCarthy remarks, 'What is needed is a sociology of faith.'[34] In this study what I have tried to offer is a christological sociology of Christian faith. Because of what God in Christ appears to be doing (taking a variety of social

---

[32] Methodists should know this, but Bonhoeffer's encounter with Methodism being alluded to here was not, of course, a favourable one (see, e.g., *Letters*, p. 341). Bonhoeffer saw Methodism as a dangerous combination of Pietist individualism and activism. His comments reflect the opposition of any sound Lutheran to Methodism's tendency to promote activist measures, rather than celebrate the generous and unearned grace of God.

[33] In a beautifully apposite insight, Wenger comments: 'One can attempt to institutionalize a community of practice, but the community of practice itself will slip through the cracks and remain distinct from its institutionalization' (*Communities of Practice*, p. 229). This insight applies, of course, to all of the institutional versions of the social forms of Christ considered throughout this study.

[34] McCarthy, *Sex and Love*, p. 217. McCarthy's book appeared when the ideas contained in this present book were well developed. Readers will be able to see many points of overlap, despite the fact that McCarthy writes as an ethicist out of a different Christian tradition (Roman Catholicism). He and I clearly share a deep conviction about the importance of theological reflection upon domestic life.

forms) I have argued that a Christology of social living (and not merely of Christian social living) is needed. It has been necessary to look at how human persons are formed in communal contexts, and to examine what this means for Christology. It will be for others to judge whether I have adequately addressed the agenda left unfinished by Bonhoeffer. But at least I have endeavoured to show how and where Christ is present, and what, in the world, in the form of person-forming human communities of practice, God appears to be doing.

Epilogue

In this Epilogue I offer a simple commentary on what I think I have been up to across the two books recording the results of my decade-long enquiry into Christocentrism in Christian practice. Whether I *can* accurately identify what I have been up to is a moot point, of course. But I present here at least what I think I have been doing. It is a personal epilogue rather than an academic summary or reflection.

Domesticity

In autumn 2000, when I began my half-time job as Faith and Order Committee Secretary for the Methodist Church in Great Britain, I introduced myself to the committee (of which I had not been a member before) as 'primarily a father'. In fact, one of the attractions of taking up the part-time post was that it would enable me to be flexible in my own work and be around more at home, permitting my wife to flourish in her full-time vocation as a Methodist minister. (Jill took up her first full-time circuit appointment in the summer of 1997.) I would try to continue to read, write and attend the odd conference to keep in touch with academic life, and perhaps do some university teaching, if any were available, alongside my half-time church appointment. But this would all have to fit around my primary role: as a father.

That is how it has been ever since. For most of the time of working on this book, 'home' has been a primary social context for me. Though I have done much more academy-related work than I expected (and have been able to do more as our children have got older), I have remained for most of the time the one who is more usually at home. I therefore continue to be empowered, frustrated, enlivened, constrained, made secure, stretched to breaking point, uplifted, enraged, and much else besides, by the joys and stresses of family life. There is no escaping the fact that this is the main context out of which I have worked, thought and written over the past eight years: more important than church and academy or any other social group.

'Domesticity' is therefore not a dirty word for me. It is my life. I am sensitive to, and usually deeply critical of, the glib remarks of theologians who speak of the 'domestication' of ideas, or of God, as if this were a bad thing. I know what they mean (for God is not to be tamed). But as family life is my primary world, I do not hear 'domestication' as 'taming' or 'reducing'. For me, domestication means bringing discussion of God into the fraught restlessness and massive extremes which are inherent in domestic life. I do not think that is what most writers mean, though, when they use the term.

My theological reflections on family life in this study are hard-won. However, it was easy to recognize that person-forming in family life is christologically significant. Whether this then led me to spin theology thinly around personal experience others must judge. I prefer to see it otherwise: family life is one of the five anvils (along with friendships, work, education and church, of course) on which my theology has been battered into shape. And it would not be theology if I thought I was always holding the hammer.

Imagination

When the children have been at school, and I have not been at my own office, or elsewhere as part of my job, I have had time to muse: clawing crucial hours from the relatively few which seem to be available ('Agh, is that the time, they'll be home from school soon!'). At those times I have been able to delve deep into the questions which have preoccupied me for years, brought together at the start of *Christ in Focus* (and quoted in the Preface to this book).

All the time I was conscious that to address these questions was no dispassionate enquiry. Academic interest and daily living were interwoven. But despite the domestic intensity out of which my recent writings have emerged, I have had to face the question whether too much of my time has been spent living theologically in my head. Also, because of the content of this present study, I need to face my own challenge and ask whether too much of my theology is rather individualistically constructed, still owing too little to the corporate contexts in which I deem that Christ is really present.

That said, it has become glaringly apparent to me throughout the writing of *Christ in Focus* and *Christ in Practice* that imagination, vision and fantasy really are very important indeed for human living, and religions must neither be sniffy about these concepts nor underestimate their dangers.

There has been a genuine sense, as I have undertaken the work, that I have been exploring an imagined world. All talk about Christ looks into the future in that it imagines how life (this life) could be, if we took the envisioned (eschatological, reign-of-God shaped) future seriously *now*. Therefore, critical studies in Christology, and of what work, education, families, friendships and church might be about in the light of Christ are always at the same time studies both of what Christ and people are and what they can become. This makes the Christians who do the imagining 'fantasists'. I have simply been among them, imagining what life could be like, using Christian resources and experience in order to do the task. Like all Christians, I must hope that in living in another world I have not left this one wholly behind.

Religion at its best is escapism of the right kind: renewal, re-creation, being resourced. Realistically, this book will not reach many people who are not already Christian, or at least religious. But if the imagined world, presented here in highly analytical form, proves to be the right kind of fantasy, then it really does matter that it begin to influence how people behave, how they critically 'read' their lives and how they contribute to the shaping of the communities and societies of which they are a part. That's how religions work, is it not? In this sense, this work of practical theology is also missiology. For at its best theology is always also missiology. This is also why systematic theologians should do more to ensure that their work is comprehensible more widely than to their own kind.

Lay spirituality

And then there's the lay thing. I do my best not to be a tub-thumping lay person. I am, after all, married to a presbyter, and so receive many of the benefits given to ministers anyway (above all a share of a house bigger than we would ever be able to afford). But being lay is important and I have been forced to conclude that lay people really do have a quite different perspective on human life from many who write theology books.

One aspect of my current job is to talk and write about 'ministry'. I had expected to do a good deal of this, but the scale on which it has actually happened has still surprised me. And this has got me thinking more broadly. Is it because of the necessity or desire within churches to review their forms of ministry so often, and because lots of theology is written by bishops and priests/presbyters/ministers (and sometimes deacons), that so much of what is published gravitates towards ecclesiology? Presbyters really do have a distinct view of the world. They do not need to be terribly 'priestly' to be like this. But they have a church-focused job to do, and people treat them in a particular kind of way. Being ordained clearly has an effect, and it can make some people more preoccupied by 'church' than may be humanly healthy. As a lay person I can hide more easily, go incognito, and even listen to the comments made about ministers. In my church job, I also have to receive roundly unjust diatribes against ministers (particularly interesting when people think I am one). What I have tried to do in this book is to turn my experience into a positive result and say what Christology looks like from a lay perspective. I have tried to offer an interpretation of Christ which is less church-focused than is usually the case. I think that is being true to Christ.

The politics of Christ-mysticism

Finally, where do I think I've ended up after this two-volume enquiry? Both terms in the heading above are crucial: 'politics' and 'Christ-mysticism'. Mysticism may seem a strange term to introduce at such a late stage in the study. It is not one I have used or argued for. It is therefore perhaps misleading to mention it now. Yet it seems to capture well my way of understanding Christ. That is, the presence of Christ is to be understood as a mystical presence in and through the complexities of human relating found in families/households, friendships, work teams, educational groups and churches in which persons are in the process of being formed through inter-subjective interaction. Christ is really present, embodied in the groups that are made up of incomplete individuals and from which the new humanity is emerging.

In using the term 'mysticism' I am following what was recognized in Part Three of *Christ in Focus*: that Christ is always related to a spiritual experience, being a spiritual presence. By not beginning with mysticism, but first exploring the concrete social forms in which Christ appears to be present, I have demonstrated the importance of the embodiment of Christ in human relationships. I thus keep mysticism grounded. Whether the term is truly apt for what I have sought to describe and explore is for students of mysticism to decide.

Keeping mysticism grounded also means, however, that I respect the fact that Christology always has a political dimension. Whether we access the meaning, presence and activity of Christ historically (through the Jesus story or through the impact of Jesus upon the churches in any era) or seek to work back from claims of encounter with Christ in human experience today, politics is unavoidable. Christ affects and is affected by what human beings do to each other and how they structure their lives. It cannot be otherwise.

Yet there is a dangerous twist in the tale/tail here. An objection could be made to my entire thesis. I have written an argument for a christological reading of a variety of forms of social life. I have claimed that these are to be regarded as social forms of Christ, which means much more than applying Christology *to* human living. In describing work teams, educational groups, families and friendships, as well as churches, as social forms of Christ, I have maintained that we learn something of Christ through them. But I have been writing from a Christian perspective, for Christians. So, the objection may be that I have done nothing but slip into one of the very distortions of Christocentrism I identified in Chapter 3 of my first book, *Christ in Focus*. I have effortlessly asserted the superiority of Christianity over all other religions and ways of reading the world. More than that, it may be objected, I have provided a manifesto for moral fascism. I am suggesting that, in viewing the forms of human living I have studied as social forms of Christ, Christians should seek to impose this way of reading them on others.

Needless to say, I resist such an objection. But I recognize its force. Christianity's history is entangled enough already with forms of fascism, moral and otherwise, and I have no desire to extend one strand of it. Yes, it is true that I think Christians would do well to 'read' the groups to which they belong carefully as a source for learning about Christ, and not just in a utilitarian way in order to muddle through life. But the fact that such readings are *not* for ethical purposes alone goes to show that I am neither proposing moral fascism nor assuming that Christianity is superior. God in Christ is present and active in a gracious, person-forming way in groups to which we belong *before* we utter any theological word and it is our task to participate in what *God* is seeking to do in Christ in the world. For these two reasons respecting an element of givenness in theology is vital. Christians, too, have yet to discover fully who and what Christ is. We do this in trying to live as Christian people, while always being capable of discovering something new about Christ through our interactions with others.

In a practical theology seminar some years ago I referred to 'receiving Christ back from the world'. It was not a phrase I had thought up; I had pinched it from someone else. But it is one of many expressions that can be used to emphasize that Christ is not contained in or by the church, and frequently challenges us in many different contexts in daily living. A clergyman at that seminar expressed bafflement at the phrase and what I was trying to signify by it. Such a reaction showed me quite early on how easily we can become ecclesiocentric in our approach to life.

The incident also taught me how necessary it is to keep plugging away at exploring who and what Christ is, in the terms suggested throughout this study. Recognizing that we 'receive Christ back from the world' is crucial if, as Christians claim, Christ is not identical to church, and God in Christ is really present and at work in the world. In short, it is we who are to be shaped by Christ, through our discovery of Christ in and through others. As Christians we are simply not in a position to bring Christ to others. Christ is revealed through participation: our participation in the social forms in which Christ is already present, seeking to be made known and brought to completion. Demanding and complicated though it can be, this is how, in Christian under-standing, we are to live as human beings: living (in) Christ in anticipatory celebration of the new humanity which God seeks to bring about. When we live in this way in families/households, friendships and churches, in educational settings and at work, the reign of God will at least have begun to break in.

Bibliography

Agenda of the Methodist Conference, Torquay 2005, Peterborough: Methodist Publishing House.

Allen, G., 1996, *Kinship and Friendship in Modern Britain*, Oxford: Oxford University Press.

Astley, J., 1996, 'The Role of the Family in the Formation and Criticism of Faith' in S. C. Barton (ed.), 1996, *The Family in Theological Perspective*, Edinburgh: T & T Clark, pp. 187–202.

Atherton, J. (ed.), 1994, *Social Christianity: A Reader*, London: SPCK.

Atherton, J., 2000, *Public Theology for Changing Times*, London: SPCK.

Atkins, M., 2001, *Preaching in a Cultural Context*, Peterborough: Foundery Press.

Au, W., 2005, 'Holistic Spirituality' in P. Sheldrake (ed.), *The New SCM Dictionary of Christian Spirituality*, London: SCM Press, pp. 342–3.

Barrett, C. K., 1962, *The Epistle to the Romans*, London: A & C Black.

— 1971, *A Commentary on the First Epistle to the Corinthians* (2nd edn), London: A & C Black.

Barth. K., 1961, *Church Dogmatics III/4*, Edinburgh: T & T Clark.

Barton, S. C. (ed.), 1996, *The Family in Theological Perspective*, Edinburgh: T & T Clark.

— (ed.), 2003, *Holiness Past and Present*, London and New York: T & T Clark.

Begbie, J., 1991, *Voicing Creation's Praise: Towards a Theology of the Arts*, Edinburgh: T & T Clark.

Best, E., 1955, *One Body in Christ*, London: SPCK.

Bethge, E., 2000, *Dietrich Bonhoeffer: A Biography* (rev. edn), Minneapolis: Fortress Press.

Bonhoeffer, D., 1954, *Life Together* (7th impression: 1968), London: SCM Press.

— 1955, *Ethics*, London: SCM Press.

— 1959, *The Cost of Discipleship*, London: SCM Press.

— 1962, *Act and Being*, London: Collins.

— 1965, *No Rusty Swords: Letters, Lectures and Notes 1928–1936*, London: Collins.

— 1966, *The Way to Freedom: Letters, Lectures and Notes 1935–1939*, London Collins.

— 1971, *Letters and Papers from Prison: The Enlarged Edition*, London: SCM Press.

— 1978, (Lectures on) *Christology*, London: Fount Paperbacks.

— 1998, *Sanctorum Communio: A Theological Study of the Sociology of the Church* (*Dietrich Bonhoeffer Works, Volume 1*), Minneapolis; Fortress Press.

Borrowdale, A., 1994, *Reconstructing Family Values*, London: SPCK.

— 1996, 'Right Relations: Forgiveness and Family Life' in S. C. Barton (ed.), *The Family in Theological Perspective*, Edinburgh: T & T Clark, pp. 203–17.

Brewer, S., 2000, '"Who Do You Say I Am?" Jesus, Gender and the Working Class Family Romance' in S. R. Munt (ed.), *Cultural Studies and the Working Class: Subject to Change*, London and New York: Cassell, pp. 167–79.

Brock, R. N., 1988, *Journeys by Heart: A Christology of Erotic Power*, New York: Crossroad.

Brown, D. and Loades A. (eds), 1996, *Christ: The Sacramental Word – Incarnation, Sacrament and Poetry*, London: SPCK.

Brown, F. B., 2000, *Good Taste, Bad Taste and Christian Taste, Aesthetics in Religious Life*, Oxford: Oxford University Press.

Browning, D., Miller-McLemore, B. J., Couture, P., Lyon, B. and Franklin, R. M., 1997, *From Culture Wars to Common Ground: Religion and the American Family Debate*, Louisville: Westminster John Knox Press.

Bruner, J., 1996, *The Culture of Education*, Cambridge, Mass. and London: Harvard University Press.

Buxton, G., 2005, 'The Failure of Functional Theologies of Ministry and the Promise of a Relational Alternative', *Ecclesiology* 1/3, pp. 27–43.

Capps, D., 1983, *Life Cycle Theory and Pastoral Care*, Philadelphia: Fortress Press.

— 2002, *Men and Their Religion: Honor, Hope, and Humor*, Harrisburg: Trinity Press International.

Carmichael, E. D. H. (Liz), 2004, *Friendship: Interpreting Christian Love*, London and New York: T & T Clark.

Catechism, 1994, *Catechism of the Catholic Church*, London: Geoffrey Chapman.

Clapp, R., 1993, *Families at the Crossroads: Beyond Traditional and Modern Options*, Downers Grove, IL and Leicester: InterVarsity Press.

Cohen, D. and Prusak, L., 2001, *In Good Company: How Social Capital Makes Organizations Work*, Boston, MA.: Harvard Business School Press.

Cone, J., 1975, *God of the Oppressed*, New York: Seabury Press.

Crossan, J. D., 1991, *The Historical Jesus: The Life of a Mediterranean Jewish Peasant*, San Francisco: HarperSan Francisco.

— 1994, *Jesus: A Revolutionary Biography*, San Francisco: HarperSanFrancisco.

Day, T., 1982, *Dietrich Bonhoeffer on Christian Community and Common Sense*, Lewiston: The Edwin Mellen Press.

De Gruchy, J. (ed.),1997, *Bonhoeffer for a New Day*, Grand Rapids: Eerdmans.

— (ed.), 1999, *The Cambridge Companion to Dietrich Bonhoeffer*, Cambridge: Cambridge University Press.

Duck, S., 1999, *Relating to Others* (2nd edn), Buckingham and Philadelphia: Open University Press.

Duffy, E., 2003, 'Scandal in the Church: Some Bearings from History', *Priests and People*, March issue.

Dunn, J. D. G., 1998, *The Theology of Paul the Apostle*, Edinburgh: T & T Clark.

Dyrness, W., 2001, *Visual Faith: Art, Theology and Worship in Dialogue*, Grand Rapids: Baker Academic.

Feil, E., 1985, *The Theology of Dietrich Bonhoeffer*, Philadelphia: Fortress Press.

Fergusson, D., 1998, *Community, Liberalism and Christian Ethics*, Cambridge: Cambridge University Press.

Fiorenza, E. Schüssler, 1999, 'To Follow the Vision: The Jesus Movement as Basileia Movement' in M. A. Farley and S. Jones (eds), *Liberating Eschatology: Essays in Honor of Letty M. Russell*, Louisville: Westminster John Knox Press, pp. 123–43.

Ford, D. F., 1999, *Self and Salvation: Being Transformed*, Cambridge: Cambridge University Press.

— 2003, 'Bonhoeffer, Holiness and Ethics' in S. C. Barton (ed.), *Holiness Past and Present*, London and New York: T & T Clark, pp. 361–80.

Fowl, S. E. and Jones, L. G., 1991, *Reading in Communion: Scripture and Ethics in Christian Life*, London: SPCK.

Fromm, E., 1963, 'The Dogma of Christ' (1930) in *The Dogma of Christ and Other Essays*, London: Routledge & Kegan Paul, pp. 1–69.

Fukuyama, F., 1996, *Trust: The Social Virtues and the Creation of Prosperity*, London: Penguin Books.

— 1999, *The Great Disruption: Human Nature and the Reconstitution of Social Order*, London: Profile Books.

Gabriel, Y., 2000, *Storytelling in Organizations: Facts, Fictions and Fantasies*, Oxford: Oxford University Press.

Green, C., 1972, *The Sociality of Christ and Humanity: Dietrich Bonhoeffer's Early Theology 1927–1933*, Missoula: Scholars Press.

Green, W., 1984, *The Future of the Family*, London: Mowbray.

Griffith, C. M., 2005, 'Education and Spirituality' in P. Sheldrake (ed.), *The New SCM Dictionary of Christian Spirituality*, London: SCM Press, pp. 266–7.

Gustafson, J. M., 1968, *Christ and the Moral Life*, Chicago and London: The University of Chicago Press.

Hanh, T. N., 1995, *Living Buddha, Living Christ*, London: Rider.

Hardy, D. W., 1989, 'Created and Redeemed Sociality' in C. Gunton and D. W. Hardy (eds.), *On Being the Church: Essays on the Christian Community*, Edinburgh: T & T Clark, pp. 21–47, reprinted in D. W. Hardy, *God's Ways with the World: Thinking and Practising Christian Faith*, Edinburgh: T & T Clark, 1996, pp. 188–205.

—1996, *God's Ways with the World: Thinking and Practising Christian Faith*, Edinburgh: T & T Clark.

Harries, R., 2003, 'Art' in J. L. Houlden (ed.), *Jesus in History, Thought and Culture: An Encyclopedia Vol. 1*, Santa Barbara, Denver, Oxford: ABC Clio, pp. 66–106.

Hauerwas, S., 1981, *A Community of Character: Toward a Constructive Christian Social Ethic*, Notre Dame and London: University of Notre Dame Press.

Hodgson, P. C., 1988, *Revisioning the Church: Ecclesial Freedom in the New Paradigm*, Philadelphia: Fortress Press.

— 1989, *God in History: Shapes of Freedom*, Nashville: Abingdon Press.

— 1994, *Winds of the Spirit: A Constructive Christian Theology*, Louisville: Westminster/John Knox Press; London: SCM Press.

Hooker, M. D., 1991, *The Gospel According to St. Mark*, London: A & C Black.

Hopper, D. W., 1975, *A Dissent on Bonhoeffer*, Philadelphia: The Westminster Press.

Hunsinger, D. van Deusen, 2000, 'Forgiving Abusing Parents: Psychological and Theological Considerations' paper presented to the Society for the Study of Theology, Oxford, 10–13 April, unpublished.

Hunt, M. E., 1992, *Fierce Tenderness: A Feminist Theology of Friendship*, New York: Crossroad.

Hurtado, L. W., 1988, *One God One Lord: Early Christian Devotion and Ancient Jewish Monotheism*, London: SCM Press.

Hurtado, L. W., 2003, *Lord Jesus Christ: Devotion to Jesus in Earliest Christianity*, Grand Rapids: Eerdmans.

Kam-Weng, N., 1996, *From Christ to Social Practice: Christological Foundations for Social Practice in the Theologies of Albrecht Ritschl, Karl Barth and Jürgen Moltmann*, Hong Kong: Alliance Bible Seminary.

Käsemann, E., 1971, 'The Theological Problem Presented by the Motif of the Body of Christ' in *Perspectives on Paul*, London: SCM Press, pp. 102–21.

Kilby, K., 2000, 'Perichoresis and Projection: Problems with the Social Doctrines of the Trinity', *New Blackfriars* 81, issue 956, October.

Knox, J., 1963, *The Church and the Reality of Christ*, London: Collins.

Lave, J. and Wenger, E., 1991, *Situated Learning: Legitimate Peripheral Participation*, Cambridge: Cambridge University Press.

Lohfink, G., 1985, *Jesus and Community*, London: SPCK.

Lohse, B., 1999, *Martin Luther's Theology: Its Historical and Systematic Development*, Edinburgh: T & T Clark.

McCarthy, D. Matzko, 2001, *Sex and Love in the Home*, London: SCM Press.

Mackey, J. P., 1994, *Power and Christian Ethics*, Cambridge: Cambridge University Press.

McLaren, B., 2004, *A Generous Orthodoxy*, Grand Rapids: Zondervan.

Marsh, C., 2002, 'Religion and the Arts' in C. Partridge (ed.), *Dictionary of Contemporary Religion in the Western World*, Leicester and Downers Grove: InterVarsity Press, pp. 65–8.

— 2003, '"Who are you for?" I Cor. 1.10–17 as Christian Scripture in the Context of Diverse Methods of Reading' in T. J. Burke and J. K. Elliott (eds.), *Paul and the Corinthians*, Leiden: Brill, pp.157–76.

— 2004, *Cinema and Sentiment: Film's Challenge to Theology*, Milton Keynes: Paternoster Press.

— 2005, *Christ in Focus: Radical Christocentrism in Christian Theology*, London: SCM Press.

— 2006, 'Diverse Agendas at Work in the Jesus Quest' in T. Holmen and S. Porter (eds.), *Handbook of the Study of the Historical Jesus: Vol. II*, Leiden: Brill.

Martin, D. B., 1990, *Slavery as Salvation: The Metaphor of Slavery in Pauline Christianity*, New Haven and London: Yale University Press.

Meilaender, G., 1981, *Friendship: A Study in Theological Ethics*, London and Notre Dame: University of Notre Dame Press.

Methodist Worship Book, 1999, Peterborough: Methodist Publishing House.

Miller-McLemore, B. J., 1994, *Also a Mother: Work and Family as Theological Dilemma*, Nashville: Abingdon Press.

Moltmann, J., 1977, *The Church in the Power of the Spirit*, London: SCM Press.

Moltmann-Wendel, E., 2000, *Rediscovering Friendship*, London: SCM Press.

Morisy, A., 2004, *Journeying Out: A New Approach to Christian Mission*, London, New York and Harrisburg: Morehouse.

Moxnes, H., 2003, *Putting Jesus in His Place: A Radical Vision of Household and Kingdom*, Louisville and London: Westminster John Knox Press.

Murphy, D. D., 2002, 'Community, Character, and Gender: Women and the Work of Stanley Hauerwas', *Scottish Journal of Theology* 55, pp. 338–55.

Nelson, J., 1992, *The Intimate Connection*, London: SPCK.

Neville, R. C., 2001, *Symbols of Jesus: A Christology of Symbolic Engagement*, Cambridge: Cambridge University Press.

Nicholls, D., 1989, *Deity and Domination: Images of God and the State in the Nineteenth and Twentieth Centuries*, London and New York: Routledge.

Nye, R., 2005, 'Adolescents and Spirituality' in P. Sheldrake (ed.), *The New SCM Dictionary of Christian Spirituality*, London: SCM Press, pp. 85–6.

Page, R., 1991, *The Incarnation of Freedom and Love*, London: SCM Press.

Parsons, S., 1996, 'Feminism and the Family' in S. C. Barton (ed.), *The Family in Theological Perspective*, Edinburgh: T & T Clark, pp. 273–90.

Pattison, S., 1996, 'Should Pastoral Care Have Aims and Objectives?', *Contact* 120, pp. 26–34.

— 2001, 'Mend the Gap: Christianity and the Emotions', *Contact* 134, pp. 3–9.

Pelikan, J., 1985, *Jesus through the Centuries*, London and New Haven: Yale University Press.

Peterson, G. R., 2003, *Minding God: Theology and the Cognitive Sciences*, Minneapolis: Fortress Press.

Phillips, J. A., 1967, *The Form of Christ in the World: A Study of Bonhoeffer's Christology*, London: Collins.

Rasmussen, L., 1999, 'The Ethics of Responsible Action' in J. De Gruchy (ed.), *The Cambridge Companion to Dietrich Bonhoeffer*, Cambridge: Cambridge University Press, pp. 206–25.

Ringe, S. H., 1999, *Wisdom's Friends: Community and Christology in the Fourth Gospel*, Louisville: Westminster John Knox Press.

Roth, W.-M., 1999, 'Authentic School Science: Intellectual Traditions' in R.

McCormick and C. Paechter (eds.), *Learning and Knowledge*, London: Paul Chapman Publishing, pp. 6–20.

Rüegger, H., 1992, *Kirche als seelsorgerliche Gemeinschaft: Dietrich Bonhoeffers Seelsorgeverständnis im Kontext seiner bruderschaftlichen Ekklesiologie*, Bern: Peter Lang.

Sanders, E. P., 1985, *Jesus and Judaism*, London: SCM Press.

Schmidt, T. E., 1987, *Hostility to Wealth in the Synoptic Gospels*, Sheffield: Sheffield Academic Press.

Simmonds, G., 2005, 'Formation, Spiritual' in P. Sheldrake (ed.), *The New SCM Dictionary of Christian Spirituality*, London: SCM Press, pp. 309–10.

Song, C. S., 1993, 'Oh, Jesus, Here with Us!' in R. S. Sugirtharajah (ed.), *Asian Faces of Jesus*, Maryknoll: Orbis; London: SCM Press, pp. 131–48.

Soosten, J. von, 1992, *Die Sozialität der Kirche: Theologie und Theorie der Kirche in Dietrich Bonhoeffers 'Sanctorum Communio'*, München: Kaiser.

Spohn, W. C., 1999, *Go and Do Likewise: Jesus and Ethics*, New York: Continuum.

Stuart, E., 1995, *Just Good Friends*, London: Mowbray.

Sykes, S. W., 1996, 'Ritual and the Sacrament of the Word' in D. Brown and A. Loades (eds.), *Christ the Sacramental Word: Incarnation, Sacrament and Poetry*, London: SPCK, pp157–67.

Talbert, C. H., 1987, *Reading Corinthians*, London: SPCK.

Thiel, J. E., 1994, *Nonfoundationalism*, Minneapolis: Fortress Press.

Thistlethwaite, S. B., 1989, *Sex, Race and God*, New York: Crossroad.

Thomas, D., 1979, *The Face of Christ*, London, New York, Sydney, Toronto: Hamlyn.

Thompson, D., 2004, *Crossing the Divide: Luther, Feminism and the Cross*, Minneapolis: Augsburg Fortress.

Thrall, M. E., 1965, *I and II Corinthians*, Cambridge: Cambridge University Press.

Time for Action, 2002, *Time for Action: Sexual Abuse, the Churches and a New Dawn for Survivors*, London: Churches Together in Britain and Ireland.

Tillich, P., 1978, *Systematic Theology 3: Life and the Spirit, History and the Kingdom of God*, London: SCM Press (originally published 1963).

Tinsley, E. J. ,1960, *The Imitation of God in Christ*, London: SCM Press.

The Virginia Report, 1997, *The Virginia Report: The Report of the Inter-Anglican Theological and Doctrinal Commission*, London: Anglican Consultative Council.

Wagner, F., 1989, 'Christologie als exemplarische Theorie des Selbstbewußtseins' in *Was ist Theologie?*, Gütersloh: Gütersloher Verlagshaus Gerd Mohn, pp. 309–42.

Ward, K., 2000, *Religion and Community*, Oxford: Clarendon Press.

Watson, N., 1992, *The First Epistle to the Corinthians*, Peterborough: Epworth Press.

Webb-Mitchell, B. P., 2003, *Christly Gestures: Learning to be Members of the Body of Christ*, Grand Rapids and Cambridge: Eerdmans.

Wenger, E., 1998, *Communities of Practice: Learning, Meaning, and Identity*, Cambridge: Cambridge University Press.

Wenger, E., McDermott, R. and Snyder, W. M., 2002, *Cultivating Communities of Practice*, Boston, MA.: Harvard Business School Press.

Whiteley, D. E. H., 1980, *The Theology of St Paul* (2nd edn), Oxford: Blackwell.

Wilkinson, H. (ed.), 2000, *Family Business*, London: Demos.

Williams, R., 2000, *On Christian Theology*, Oxford and Malden: Blackwell.

Willmer, H., 2000, 'Jesus Christ the Forgiven: Christology, Atonement and Forgiveness', paper presented to the Society for the Study of Theology, Oxford, 10–13 April, unpublished.

Zerner, R., 1999, 'Church, State and the "Jewish Question"' in J. De Gruchy (ed.), *The Cambridge Companion to Dietrich Bonhoeffer*, Cambridge: Cambridge University Press.

Index